CONTEMPORARY APPALACHIA: IN SEARCH OF A USABLE PAST

*Proceedings of the
Ninth Annual
Appalachian Studies Conference*

Edited by:
CARL ROSS

Managing Editor:
JANE SHOOK

The Appalachian Consortium was a non-profit educational organization composed of institutions and agencies located in Southern Appalachia. From 1973 to 2004, its members published pioneering works in Appalachian studies documenting the history and cultural heritage of the region. The Appalachian Consortium Press was the first publisher devoted solely to the region and many of the works it published remain seminal in the field to this day.

With funding from the Andrew W. Mellon Foundation and the National Endowment for the Humanities through the Humanities Open Book Program, Appalachian State University has published new paperback and open access digital editions of works from the Appalachian Consortium Press. For more information visit:
http://www.collections.library.appstate.edu/appconsortiumbooks.

ISBN (pbk.: alk. Paper): 978-1-4696-3678-8
ISBN (epub ebook): 978-1-4696-3679-5
ISBN (updf ebook): 978-1-4696-3680-1

Distributed by the University of North Carolina Press
www.uncpress.org

Table of Contents

1986 PROGRAM COMMITTEE
Carl Ross, Chair

Patricia Beaver
Laura Binder
Richard Blaustein
Barry Buxton
Clay Estepp
Mike Kline
Parks Lanier

Ruby Lanier
Gordon McKinney
Mike Mullins
Karl Raitz
Helen Roseberry
James Sessions
Jim Stone

Introduction

The Appalachian Studies Association was formed in 1977 by scholars, teachers and regional activists who believed that a shared community of ideas and interests had been and would continue to be important for those writing, researching and teaching about things Appalachian. The first Appalachian Studies Conference was held at Berea, Kentucky in March of 1978.

We have learned much since that first conference. We now more fully realize how dynamic Appalachian society has always been. Today, we can see that there has long been a reciprocal interaction between the Appalachian region and the larger American society.

All of us make judgements and decisions based on what has gone before. The better our understanding of these past events, the more we are able to act with intelligence and sensitivity in the present. No one can understand his society without a comprehension of its evolution. Understanding our past will not always explain everything we want to know about our current state of affairs, but it can help us to make sense out of many matters which are otherwise bewildering and remind us that although we live in a complex era, previous generations have confronted equal complexities.

Knowledge of the past can be a source of consolation in a bewildering world. We must be careful not to accept present institutions and policies as the best and wisest, but neither should we reject them out of hand. By drawing upon the perspectives of the past, we can approach the present with greater sensitivity. Conversely, we will never understand our present or be able to deal with the future unless we can in some way make sense of our past, learn its lessons, and use that knowledge to shape our future.

The 1986 Program Committee chose to direct its attention to contemporary Appalachia and to focus on our search for a usable past. In doing so, we affirmed our belief that a better understanding of our past will enhance our sense of identity, show that we are products of our own culture, enable us to learn from our past, understand our present, and shape our future.

The papers included in this publication are a representative sampling of those presented at the conference. Budgetary and editorial considerations precluded the inclusion of many other papers. It is our hope that this volume will contribute to a wider understanding of our region.

Carl A. Ross, Chair
1986 Program Committee

The Search For Community In Appalachia

by
Ron D. Eller
University of Kentucky

The mountains have much to share with the rest of the country. The story of the mountains is the story of the nation writ small. It is the story of man's relationship to the land, of man's relationship to man—exploitation, racism, sexism, conflict, despair, pride, and triumph. It is the story of democratic people struggling with mass culture, mass thinking, capitalism, and individualism.

In recent years we Americans generally have expressed growing concern about the decline of "community" in our land. Such diverse writers as Simone Weil, Christopher Lasch, Peter Berger, Wendell Barry, and a host of others have lamented the individualizing tendencies of modern culture and have called for a revival of community structures that once provided the safety net for most Americans.[1] The "Roots" phenomenon of the 1970s reflected as much a desire for conectedness in our present lives as it did a desire to rediscover our ancestors. Recently, Robert Bellah and his associates have renewed the debate over our national character with their best seller, *Habits of the Heart*.[2]

We in Appalachian studies should be doubly interested in this debate since the search for community has been central to our work in the region for many years. No theme has been stronger in our literature than the effort to understand the Appalachian character and to explain the nature of the mountain community. If we agree with John Stephenson that Appalachian studies is as much a social movement as an academic enterprise, then that movement itself emerged out of our collective concern for the survival of the mountain community.[3] From another perspective, it is our common search for roots and for meaningful relationships in a rootless society that brings us all together as the Appalachian studies community.

Certainly, no aspect of mountain life has been so frequently studied and yet so misunderstood and maligned as "community." In fact, for over a hundred years observers of mountain life have denied the existence of "community" altogether in our region. Emma Bell Miles, who was otherwise a perspective observer, wrote in 1905 that "there is no such thing as a community of mountaineers. They are knit together, man to man, as friends, but not as a body of men...."[4] Writers from that time to the present—including Horace Kephart, Samuel Tyndale Wilson,

James Watt Raine, Jack Weller, Rupert Vance, Thomas R. Ford, and many others—have continued that traditionals view. Jack Weller summarized their attitudes: he wrote in 1965 that the mountaineers "have no community life as such or life outside their very limited family group.... They are virtually impossible to organize into groups and are traditionalistic in the extreme."[5]

Given this perceived absence of community, John C. Campbell concluded that the dominant trait of the mountaineer was independence, "independence raised to the fourth power.... Heredity and environment," he wrote, "have conspired to make (the mountaineer) an extreme individualist."[6] Campbell devoted an entire chapter in his classic book to the individualism of the Southern highlanders, and almost every writer since has found individualism to be one of the most powerful, definable traits of "mountain character." According to this received vision, *the mountaineer is the extreme individualist* who cares nothing for cooperation and has no commitment to community beyond what he can get out of it for himself.

This notion of mountain individualism has provided grist for the theoretical mill of those who would see the region as uncivilized, backward, barbaric or degenerate. It has become the popular symbol of the mountaineer in cartoons and the media and has been used to explain everything from labor violence to poor health. In fact, the origins of this individualistic image are deeply rooted in the "idea of Appalachia" itself and lie entwined in the work of turn of the century writers who associated individualism with the passing frontier and community with the progressive and civilizing forces of modern, urban life. Campbell, for example, drew his accounts of the early history of Appalachia from the work of Theodore Roosevelt and Frederick Jackson Turner, men who believed that the frontier had been an individualizing experience, one which had given rise to the great independent spirit of American democracy.[7]

More recent historians, however, have all but turned the "Frontier Thesis" on its head and have pointed to the persistence of community in the westward movement rather than to settlement by independent pioneers. Far from being extreme individualists forced to adapt to a harsh environment, the early frontiersmen were more likely to be part of an extended community of interdependent families, and by practicing communal and cooperative efforts they were able not only to survive but to flourish. Contemporary scholars associate the rise of individualism with the growth of capitalism and modernization, not with the persistence of the frontier.[8] Unfortunately this scholarship has had little effect upon Appalachian studies, and the communal heritage in the mountain character has been all but lost to our collective memory.

Research into the nature of the mountain community, therefore, would undoubtedly reveal a split tradition. In Appalachia, like the rest of

4

the country, individualism and commitment have both been part of our common heritage. As Robert Bellah and others have argued, Americans have always spoken a dual language—one rooted in images of radical individualism, private achievement, personal consumption, and individual success; the other in images of civic responsibility, social equality, public virtue, and commitment. This second, public language was central to the republican tradition that dominated the early years of our history, while the voice of individualism emerged to dominate the cultural revolution that accompanied the rise of modern capitalism.[9]

Many contemporary observers of American society believe that this first language of individualism has so displaced our second language of civic virtue that it is undermining our capacity for commitment to one another and threatens the very fiber of our democratic life. "Almost all Americans in the 1980s," writes Harry Boyte, "have experienced some form of wrenching detachment from the communal settings that might nourish a deep and continuous sense of what it means to be an American."[10] Expressive individualism, these critics believe, not only saps us of the connectedness necessary for personal identity, but it weakens the social values of cooperation and responsibility necessary for a democratic society. Individualism separates us from the society around us and causes us to forget our ancestors, to forget our traditions, and to imagine that our whole destiny is in our own hands. We live for the present, lack concern for the well-being of others, and base our actions upon how we feel at the moment because we have little understanding of how others before us have acted. Like Jim Wayne Miller's Brier, "we don't know any more about our history than a dog knows his daddy.... We try to live in somebody else's house....(We're) educated, don't believe in nothing."[11]

But we in Appalachia do profess to believe in something—in our land, in our families, in our traditions, in our God, and in our sense of social justice. Perhaps that is why Appalachian studies has been throughout its history a challenge to the cultural hegemony of modern American life. It allows us to believe that we are doing more with our lives than just serving ourselves. Some of us have focused our challenge to modernism on political and economic relationships that have left our region exploited and impoverished. Others have focused criticism on the loss of certain moral values or on the modern restraints to self-expression and identity. As a result of these diverse responses to modernism, we in Appalachian studies used to divide ourselves into the "action folk" (politically oriented people) and the "creative folk" (literary and artistic people), as if knowledge, creativity, and politics were somehow separable.[12] But politics and culture are part of the same whole, and any effort to change economic conditions must be considered within a cultural context. We are all engaged in the search for purpose in our lives, in the search for rootedness that gives meaning to our work.

Roots, however, don't exist in a singular vacuum; they require commitment to others—an interconnectedness that gives life to the whole. Thus, the challenge is not simply to abandon our first language in favor of the second, our private world in favor of the public sphere, but to reorient our individual lives for the benefit of the community as a whole. Our pioneer ancestors placed a high value on self-reliance, but that self-reliance had a clearly collective context. It was as a people that they acted independently and a self-reliantly. With the rise of modernism the collective note was muted and our primary obligation has come to be to ourselves. The differences which divide us in Appalachian studies today, therefore, may have less to do with action-seeking vs. creativity than with the reasons for our involvement with this work itself and the level of our commitment to personal and collective goals.

But how do we nourish the collective spirit? For us in the mountains to renew our communities and build a more just and equitable future for our children will require a new commitment and a fundamental realignment of our values. As we have learned in recent years, Appalachia will not be rescued from the outside, whether by the federal government or the private sector. Renewal must begin from within, with the revitalization of communities and of the spirit of self-help and civic virtue. The recovery of community will require that we move beyond a defensive reaction against the things which threaten us and assume a positive initiative to create a new cultural context for democratic change. Such an initiative requires that we relearn old skills and acquire new perspectives: how to talk to each other, how to share with each other, how to recover collective memories, how to discern common values out of diverse traditions, and how to connect personal troubles with social issues.[13]

Central to this process is the restoration of our collective memory. As is true with most social movements, the first step to collective consciousness is the recovery of those common experiences and customs which grant dignity to the individual and an alternative view of the prevailing culture. Martin Luther King recognized the importance of historical memory to the civil rights movement and encouraged his followers not only to recover the lost history of blacks in America, but also to recover the lost meaning of democracy as well. For King the civil rights movement was "not only directed at the transformation of unjust structures; it was also a school for citizenship through which ordinary men and women would acquire "a new sense of somebodyness."[14] Having an understanding of how others before us have acted gives us the confidence to make decisions in the present, to create out of traditions for the past new visions for the future.

Robert Bellah consideres historical memory to be essential to community:

6

> Communities . . . have a history—in an important sense they
> are constituted by their past—and for this reason we can
> speak of a real community as a "community of memory,"
> one that does not forget its past. In order not to forget that
> past, a community is involved in retelling its story, its
> constitutive narrative, and in so doing, it offers examples of
> the men and women who have embodied and exemplified
> the meaning of the community.[15]

We in Appalachian studies have made great strides in the recovery of our collective memory, but we have far to go in beginning to share that memory with ordinary men and women in the region.

Modern culture, with its emphasis on change, has a way of robbing us of historical memory. Appalachians have been especially victimized by that tendency, and until we do a better job recovering and retelling our history, we will be unable to recognize and evaluate the alternative social visions that have existed within our past. Only then can we hope to develop an Appalachian conception of the meaning of a good life and thus an alternative vision for the future.

Recovering our collective memory will also help us to learn once again to talk to each other, to share with each other, and to discern our common values. As the oral history students of the 1970's learned, recording the oral traditions of their neighbors required more than mechanical skills. It taught them how to communicate and how to listen, how to think across time, and how to relate the lives of individuals to the larger social order. Above all it gave them insight into the lives of the men and women who sustained them. In the process, they became tied to that community of memory themselves.

Renewing our individual ties to our communities of memory is a further step toward building active, democratic citizenship. Classical republicanism evoked an image of the active citizen contributing to the public good, and this. notes Bellah, requires us to see the individual within the context of the larger community rather than seeing the "self" as "the only or main form of reality."[16] Remembering our heritage involves accepting our origins—including the painful memories of prejudice, poverty, and exploitation that the pressures to modernize have attempted to deny. Accepting these painful memories is often the wellspring for social consciousness. Thus leaving behind one kind of individualism, Bellah suggests, will help us acquire a new civic individualism, that entails care for the affairs of the community and a new definition of the relationship of individuals to society.

Let us take, for example, the meaning of work in our modern world. How does the way that we define work affect our relationship to community? How does the way in which we in Appalachian studies define our roles as scholars, teachers, and activists affect our ability to relate to mountain communities and mountain people? When I was growing up, I was encouraged to "make something of myself" by moving beyond my raising, beyond my family and the cultural community of which I was a part. Success was defined by my teachers as moving up the economic and social ladder, escaping the hillbilly world of "yesterday's people." Education became the utilitarian route to getting a job, and work became simply a way of making money and achieving personal success.

Gone from this modern, individualistic notion of work is the older sense of work as a "calling," wherein one's work was morally inseparable from the needs of the community. In pre-industrial mountain communities, work was a moral relationship between people not just a source of material or personal reward. The work of each person contributed to the good of the whole, and the success of that work was judged by its contribution to the success of the community rather than what the individual could get out of it. I wonder to what extent those of us in Appalachian studies today feel this sense of our work as commitment to that larger community which we profess to study or to what extent we simply use that community to further our own careers and institutional goals or to test our most recent intellectual theory. Is our work in Appalachian studies defined in terms of self-fulfillment or in terms of its contribution to the common good?

If we are to be about the business of nourishing community in our society, we must be more than just a gathering of like-minded individuals whose union depends entirely on spontaneous interest. We must carry a shared sense of civic virtue and committed citizenry into our classrooms and into the communities in which we live and work. We must recognize the many forms of community that still survive in the mountains and support their efforts to bring dignity and meaning to the lives of mountain people: volunteer fire departments, religious organizations, self-help societies, neighborhood associations, reform groups and other associations up and down the ridge which sustain public vitality and the egalitarian spirit. Such associations challenge people to think of themselves as a community—giving, sharing, cooperating,—and they provide living demonstrations of democracy at work.[17]

As for ourselves, we must live out our own understanding of community and bring knowledge and action together in the fulfillment of our professed beliefs. If Appalachian studies is to continue to fulfill its origins as a social movement, it must sustain the power to galvanize widespread political action for reforms of the structures that threaten mountain communities. This means the revival in our own minds of the old Jeffersonian, republican notion of democratic citizenship which requires the active participation of the individual in the political life of the whole. Commitment to community requires both servanthood and servant leadership, and public virtue necessitates politcal action to right the wrongs created by the excessive exercise of private power. We who profess to believe in Appalachia must work beside our brothers and sisters in the base communities of the region to support their struggles for democracy, jobs, and a better quality of life. We serve only ourselves if we study mountain culture, write mountain history, evaluate mountain conditions without applying that knowledge to the living community and using it to shape an alternative future.

Rebuilding the community will, finally, require more from us in the future than we have provided in the past. It will mean above all that we take seriously the challenge to provide a vision of what things might become in the mountains and in the larger society. It has often been said that we in Appalachian studies have a better idea of what we are against than of what we are for. We have been quick to react to specific threats and issues, but we have been slower to build a collective vision of what life in Appalachia might become. Martin Luther King recognized the importance of vision and dreams to his people, and he constantly reminded them of that dream. King knew the meaning of that verse in Proverbs: "Where there is no vision, the people perish."[18] We might add that where there are no visionaries, the dreams perish as well.

Building a vision of an alternative future based on strong community ties will require a new kind of thinking, a new kind of mind for Americans whose culture has been so strongly shaped by modern individualism. Yet we may have within our own mountain traditions the roots from which new spiritual values may arise: ethics of respect, hard work, family, self-reliance, personal dignity, tolerance, fairness, cooperation, and democracy. Our task is to fashion these strands of individualism and community into a practical ideology that is appropriate for a new era.

Eudora Welty once observed, "One place comprehended can make us understand other places better. Sense of place gives equilibrium; extended, it is sense of direction."[19] Pehaps the search for community in Appalachia may provide a sense of direction for the rebuilding of community in America.

ENDNOTES

1. Simone Weil, *The Need For Roots*, trans. Arthur Wills (New York: Putnam, 1952); Christopher Lasch, "Mass Culture Reconsidered," in *Democracy* (October 1981); Peter Berger, *Facing Up To Modernity: Excursions Into Society, Politics and Religion* (New York: Basic, 1977); Wendell Berry, *The Unsettling of America: Culture and Agriculture* (New York: Avon Books, 1978). See also Kirkpatrick Sale, Human Scale (New York: Putnam, 1980).

2. Robert N. Bellah, et. al., *Habits of the Heart: Individualism and Commitment in American Life* (Berkeley: University of California Press, 1985).

3. See John Stephenson, "Politics and Scholarship: Appalachian Studies Enter the 1980's," *Appalachian Journal*, Vol. 9, Nos. 2 & 3 (Winter-Spring 1982), pp. 97–104.

4. Emma Bell Miles, *The Spirit of the Mountains* (Knoxville: The University of Tennessee Press, 1975), p.71.

5. Jack Weller, *Yesterday's People: Life in Contemporary Appalachia* (Lexington: University of Kentucky Press, 1965), p. 88.

6. John C. Campbell, *The Southern Highlander and His Homeland* (Lexington: The University of Kentucky Press, 1969), p. 91.

7. See for example, Campbell, *The Southern Highlander*, pp. 93–94.

8. See for example, Berger, *Facing Up To Modernity*; Rowland Berthoff, "Peasants and Artisans, Puritans and Republicans," *Journal of American History*, 69 (Winter, 1982); Craig Calhoun, "The Radicalism of Tradition: Community Strength or Venerable Disguise and Borrowed Language," *The American Journal of Sociology*, 88 (March 1983); and John Kasson, *Civilizing the Machine: Technology and Republican Values in America* (New York: Penguin, 1977).

9. Bellah et. al., *Habits of the Heart*, pp. 27–35 & 142–144.

10. Harry C. Boyte, *Community is Possible: Repairing America's Roots* (New York: Harper and Row, 1984) p. 31.

11. Jim Wayne Miller, "Brier Sermon: You Must Be Born Again" in *The Mountains Have Come Closer* (Boone, N.C.: Appalachian Consortium Press, 1980).

12. See discussions of this "division" in essays included in "Assessing Appalachian Studies," *Appalachian Journal*, Vol. 9, Nos. 2 & 3 (Winter-Spring 1982).

13. Boyte, *Community Is Possible*, p. 11.

14. Boyte, *Community Is Possible*, p. 217.

15. Bellah et. al., *Habits of the Heart*, p. 153.

16. Bellah et. al., *Habits of the Heart*, p. 143.

17. See on this subject the work of Harry Boyte and Sara Evans, *Free Spaces: The Sources of Democratic Change in America* (New York: Harper and Row, 1986) and Gar Alperovitz and Jeff Faux, *Rebuilding America* (New York: Pantheon, 1984).

18. *Proverbs* 29:18.

19. Quoted in C. Vann Woodward, "District of Devils," *The New York Review* (October 10, 1985), p. 30.

Comfort In Confinement: Gender Roles In The Old Regular Baptist Church

by
Howard Dorgan

Outside of Amish and Mennonite communities, it will be difficult to find American social orders in which gender roles are more absolute than they sometimes are in Old Regular Baptist congregations. In many of these fellowships, highly traditional models for male/female behavior, forged for the most part from Pauline biblical mandates, stand as the socially accepted paradigms for conduct in dress, speech, involvement in church governance, physical appearances, and family relationships. The result is a set of gender codes that are exceptionally confining, but which provide a few comforts in that confinement.

This paper first examines some gender-role-related actions taken in recent annual meetings of the Sardis Association of Old Regular Baptist, the Church of Jesus Christ, and the Union Association of Old Regular Baptists of Jesus Christ, actions relative to dress and hair styles permissible for women of this Baptist sect. Then examination is made of certain biblical passages employed by Old Regulars as justification for their gender codes. Next, the theme "Comfort in Confinement" is briefly explored, followed by a discussion of "cracks in the tablets," preliminary indications that even in these highly traditional fellowships some women are beginning to demand at least a small degree of liberation.

11

Sardis and Union Association Actions, 1975, 1979, 1982, and 1983

The Sardis and Union Associations, two of six such confederations of Old Regular fellowships operating in the Appalachian region[1], are composed of twenty-nine and sixty-seven churches respectively, scattered all the way from Michigan to Florida, but located primarily in western Virginia and eastern Kentucky. These fellowships exist as some of the most "old time way" religious communities in the Southern Appalachian region, preserving customs that mirror values and beliefs of the mid-nineteenth century.

Old Regular association meetings are held each year and are governed by a moderator and assistant moderator, a clerk and assistant clerk, and three delegates for each member fellowship. The role of these annual sessions is to deliberate all matters of association governance, including such behavioral codes as might be applicable to members of the affiliated fellowships.

In 1975, 1979, 1982, and 1983 the Sardis and Union Associations debated two topics relevant to the issue of gender roles in these traditional Southern Appalachian religious communities: (1) the manner of dress acceptable for women members of these fellowships, and (2) permissible hair lengths for both male and female members.

The first of these issues, the proper dress for women, has been a thorny question for years in both the Sardis and Union associations, with some member churches holding to more traditional practices than those followed by other congregations. Within the Sardis group of churches, the dispute reached a peak in 1975 when one of the more conservative fellowships, Dix Fork Church of Sidney, Kentucky, introduced the following query during that year's session: "Does the Sardis Association believe in Sisters wearing pants, slacks, or shorts?"[2]

As is usually the case in such circumstances, the Dix Fork query was first referred to a special committee, with instruction that these individuals advise the rest of the delegates as to what action should be taken. The committee in question, however, refused to recommend an absolute position, and instead threw the matter back in the hands of the individual churches:

Dingess, W.Va.
September 13, 1975

Sardis Association of
Old Regular Baptists

Brethren:

In answer to the Query from the Dix Fork Church asking "Does the Sardis Association believe in Sisters wearing pants, slacks or shorts?" We as an Advisory Council and not as a law making body say:

> To answer this Query in the affirmative would be interpreted by some Brethren too liberally and they would say we have laid down the gate and opened the doors to anything and everything.

> To answer this Query in the negative would be interpreted by some Brethren too strictly and they would say we have shut the door on everything and Committees would flow from Church to Church like water.

We believe the Sardis Association should advise the Churches to advise their members—both Brethren and Sisters—to dress soberly and modestly and to conduct themselves in a manner that becometh a Child of God. We believe that each Child of God will adorn themselves in such a manner that they can easily be identified from the World. We feel the Bible, the infallible Word of God, sets forth and the Spirit will teach us how we should dress and conduct ourselves.

We believe, and the Association has so stated in the past, that each Church in the Sardis Association holds the key to its own door and is the sole judge of the conduct of its members as long as they follow the orthodox principles of religion and keep up a Godly discipline according to the rules of the Gospel as laid down in the Scriptures. In fact, Article 3 of our

13

Constitution guarantees that the Association shall not infringe on any internal right to the Churches.

Elder Wayne Herald
Brother Ralph W. E. Varney, Jr.
Brother James M. Ray[3]

Thus, this committee advised the association not to take any action on this question but instead to allow individual churches to institute their own dress codes for female members. The "holds the key to its own door" language is very traditional in Old Regular rhetoric and always means that the individual fellowship retains the right to decide whom to include in their membership and whom to exclude. Obviously in this instance, the standard for inclusion is proper dress, and the local church is given the right to set and enforce that standard. In the 1975 debate, the Sardis Association simply accepted the special committee's report and took no further action, thus leaving the matter in the hands of local congregations.

This 1975 action, however, did not settle the issue, and the more conservative churches in the association have continued to push for an absolute code for the entire Sardis body. The result has been that twice in recent years (1982 and 1983) the session delegates have voted to republish the special committee's response to the Dix Fork query.[4]

Essentially the same dispute has erupted in the Union Association of Old Regulars. In 1979 the Little Martha congregation of Leemaster, Virginia, requested that their fellow Union Old Regular churches join them in the adoption of a rigid code for both dress and hair lengths. The Little Martha group made their request by placing the following proposal before the Union delegates:

> We the Little Martha Church of Old Regular Baptist of Jesus Christ... send a request to the Union Association not to allow Sisters to wear pants or pantsuits. We ask them to be as our Sisters of Old, only to be worn as for safety, or if they are working on a job that require them to be worn. Even at this they should be worn loose not in a way to show their bodies in an ungodly manner.
>
> We also ask that Brothers and Sisters not to wear Bathing suits or shorts for any reason, also ask the Brothers not to wear their hair long enough that it might be an offense to another Brother or Sister.
>
> We are asking that all Moderators advise their Churches that if any Brother or Sister is guilty of the above that they be advised to stop such practice and if they refuse to do so that they be excluded, until such time that they have stopped such

practice, then the Church from which they were excluded may restore them to full fellowship.

We the Little Martha Church is sending this request not to tear the Churches apart, but to try to unite them into full fellowship with each other to be united as one.

Signed by Order of the Church
Elder John C. Layne, Moderator
Elder Russell Hicks, Assistant Moderator
Brother Hufford Coleman, Clerk[5]

By a vote of one hundred and thirty-one to fifty-three the Little Martha request was denied, but the fifty-three votes in support of the motion indicate that approximately twenty-nine percent of the delegates favored very rigid dress and hair style code for Old Regular women. However, had the vote been exclusively on length of hair the support would have been much greater: In both the Sardis and the Union Associations there is broad agreement that women should not cut their hair and that men should do just the opposite.

For example, the Sardis Association reaffirmed its position on hair lengths for women in 1982 and again in 1983, passing a resolution that is not open to a wide range of interpretations: "The Association, by regular move and second, said that if a Sister cut her hair, she should be asked to let it grow out; if she fails to do so and cuts her hair again, she will be excluded."[6]

To be "excluded" means to be removed from membership in the congregation. The judgement carries with it factors of social ostracism that may become quite severe, depending upon the community involved. Nevertheless, the punishment is usually not as harsh as apparently "shunning" is within Amish communities, and does not include, for example, the mandate that the excluded individual never be addressed by any conforming and legitimate member of the fellowship.[7]

A major problem, however, relative to enforcement of the no-cutting mandate is that the rule must be interpreted. Is it permissible, for example, simply to trim one's hair—to keep the ends even and neat? Is shoulder-length hair acceptable, or must a woman allow her hair to grow as long as it will naturally grow?

A conversation with Mrs. Edwin May, wife of the moderatior of the Sardis Association, has suggested that there usually is some discretion allowed in these matters, and that most fellowships do not stand eager to reprimand and exclude at the slightest hint of scissors having touched hair.[8] Still it has been my observation that the vast majority of middle-aged and older Old Regular women allow their hair to grow long enough that it must me worn in a topknot or braided bun, and that unloosed this hair would fall to the middle of the back or lower.

Old Regular men, on the other hand, must keep their hair reasonably short, never allowing it to extend down around the lower neck or to flow over the ears in any feminine fashion. To illustrate this requirement I will tell a story about one of my favorite Old Regular elders, Bill Campbell of the Bull Creek fellowship in Maxie, Virginia.

Campbell is a relatively young elder, only in his mid-thirties. He joined the Old Regular faith at the age of twenty-nine, after several years of a life style which he now describes as having been quite depraved. In fact, when he approached an elder of the Bull Creek Church with his interest in being baptized he looked—by his own description—"a mess," possessing a full beard and a head of hair in the style of the "flower childrend" of the late '60s and early '70s. The result was that the elder refused to baptize Campbell until he had made himself more presentable to the fellowship. This did not mean that he had to shave his beard, but it did mean that his long hair had to go.[9]

Biblical Mandates for these and Other Gender Codes

Old regulars can point to a biblical passage as justification for their stances concerning the length of hair. The passage in question is 1st Corinthians 11:14–15:

> Doth not even nature itself teach you, that, if a man have long hair, it is a shame unto him?
> But if a woman have long hair, it is a glory to her; for her hair is given her for a covering. [King James Version]

This, of course, comes from the writings of Paul, the New Testament voice upon which Old Regulars most depend for guidance in gender role propriety.

Paul is also the authority upon whom these congregations rely when they hold tenaciously to a church policy that is exclusively male controlled. In 1st Corinthians 14:34–35 Paul had this to say:

> Let your women keep silence in the churches; for it is not permitted unto them to speak; but they are commanded to be under obedience, as also saith the law.
> And if they will learn anything, let them ask their husbands at home; for it is a shame for women to speak in the church.

As a result of this particular biblical passage, Old Regulars maintain church governance systems devoid of any formal female participation. This

16

does not mean, however, that women maintain total silence in Old Regular churches. They sing, shout, pray, and praise; but they play no official roles in worship procedures or in business deliberations. During formal business sessions, they have no voice or vote, and they assume no duties that place them before congregations in positions of leadership. Indeed, about the only way in which they affect church policy is through the informal influence they might bring to bear upon husbands or other male members of the family.

Even this latter option, however, is severely restricted in the more rigidly traditional Old Regular household. Here, again, the advice of Paul is followed:

> Wives, submit yourselves unto your own husbands, as unto the lord.
> For the husband is the head of the wife, even as Christ is the head of the church; and he is the savior of the body.
> Therefore, as the church is subject unto Christ, so let the wives be to their own husbands in every thing.
>
> Ephesians 5:22-24

Of course Paul added, "Husbands love your wives, even as Christ also loved the church . . . "; but he did not say, as Old Regular males observe, "Husbands, submit yourselves unto your wives." Therefore, in these very traditional Old Regular homes, the women have little more to say than they have in church, at least relative to religious doctrines or church social policies.

Old Regular fellowships do not believe in Sunday schools (or Sabbath schools as they call them), and part of the reason for this position touches on the proper role of women in church. These Old Regulars note that in other Baptist subdenominations in which Sunday schools have been instituted, it has been the women who do most of the teaching. This, of course, violates the Pauline mandate that "women should keep silence in the churches." Children, they argue, should be raised "in the nurture and admonition of the Lord [Ephesians 6:4]," but this raising should be accomplished in the home. Furthermore, Old Regular elders are quick to point to the fact that Paul said, "ye fathers . . . bring them up in the nurture and admonition of the Lord."[10] This places the primary responsibility for the spiritual upbringing of a child on the shoulders of Father, a situation quite opposite from comparable circumstances in most Protestant American homes.

17

Comfort in Confinement

My general impression of Old Regular women is that the majority of them are not particularly disturbed by the restrictions I have been discussing, that they have become more comfortable with these confinements and desire no other life style. One thing to note here is that Old Regular members tend to be quite old on the average, with the result that both males and females have settled into relatively unchanging life patterns. As significant factors in these life patterns, fixed gender models provide a form of security, firmly guiding individuals through the otherwise confused maze of life's choices.

One elderly member of the Bethany Old Regular fellowship of Kingsport, Tennessee, told me that she had absolutely no desire to complicate her life by taking on all those issues she felt belonged to men of her church: "I've got enough things to do, thank you. There are squabbles that go on in the church that I'd just as soon let the men handle. That leaves me free just to enjoy the singing and preaching."[11] In this woman's eyes, the franchise in church governance would simply be another burden to bare.

Cracks in the Tablets

Is everybody happy, however, with the rigid rules of the past? Is there no dissatisfaction among Old Regulars with the gender roles that were prescribed by Paul? The mere fact that the positions reported earlier as taken by the Dix Fork Church in the Sardis Association and the Little Martha Church in the Union Association have become minority positions would seem to suggest there has been some movement among Old Regulars towards modernism of gender roles, at least relative to clothing. That movement, however, has been slow. What could add some speed, nevertheless, would be (1) an increasing concern among Old Regular women over their gender's lack of rights, and (2) a growing awareness of was to translate this concern into protest.

I have no documentation to support a charge of some great ground swell of indignation occurring within Old Regular feminine ranks. Instead, all I have is a small amount of anecdotal evidence which may suggest the beginnings of dissatisfaction.

This first story was related to me by Darvin Marshall of St. Paul, Virginia, who became my first contact with the Sandy Ridge Old Regular Church of that vicinity. According to Marshall, during the 1979 Union Association debate over the Little Martha Church's request, a few women did not respond to the issue with total passivism. Indeed, one Sandy Ridge female, Marshall recalls, showed a strong repugnance for the reasoning of an elder who directed a scathing attack against certain items of contemporary

18

women's dress, including panty hose. This woman's response, says Marshall, was to steal into the parking area during the session, locate the respective elder's automobile, and stretch a pair of panty hose across the front windshield wipers of the vehicle, much to the later embarrassment of this conservative gentleman. [12]

My next story relates to a lengthy discussion I had, February 15, 1985, with Elder and Mrs. Edwin May. As previously noted, Elder May is Moderator of the Sardis Association. He invited me to his home in Abingdon, Virginia, for a daylong interview concerning Old Regular doctrines and various customs of the Sardis Association.

Early in our dialogue I asked about the role of women in the church and received much of the information I related above. At one point, however, I turned to Mrs. May, who sat quietly by during the entire interview, and asked her if she had any objections concerning the lack of female involvement in church business. Her response was very much in line with the one I have already related, the comments made by the Bethany Old Regular matron. Mrs. May said she had no real desire to take on all those problems.

Later, I moved in my queries to an issue which appears to have been particularly complicated for Old Regular fellowships, the question of how to handle divorced members. The precise topic being discussed was Old Regular policy governing the acceptability of divorce and remarriage, and conditions under which a divorced and remarried individual could remain in the church.

As I interviewed Elder May on these questions Mrs. May appeared to be very interested. In fact, at one point she even asked for clarification of a doctrine, suggesting by her question that she had never heard of this issue discussed before in detail. May was explaining that fellowships of the Sardis Association would not retain in membership individuals, male or female, who had "put away their companions" for any reason other than the charge of fornication. He further noted that if fornication became an issue in any particular deliberation, the charge would have to be heard in a regular business meeting of the fellowship.

It was at this point that Mrs. May seemed to have some trouble accepting the association's policy. In fact, for a moment she seemed to forget her "position," making a statement that appeared to question the propriety of such a charge being heard in an open meeting. Nevertheless, she did not push the issue.

I, on the other hand, said something that may have overstepped the decorum of the moment: I asked her if she would like to vote on this policy. For a moment she made no response, and then simply smiled, recognizing at that instance—I felt—the contradiction lying between her interest in this issue and the earlier passive position she had taken. [13]

I quickly moved away from the question, fearing that I might offend Elder May, but I had a strong feeling that I had witnessed another slight "crack in the tablet."

I do not want to suggest, however, by these two stories that radical changes are imminent, that any week, or month, or year Old Regular women will rise to the cause of women's rights. I simply do not see that happening. Traditional gender codes are just too firmly set in these fellowships. But if the Old Regular subdenomination is still around in, let's say, 2025—and I suspect it will be—some wearing away of this rock-ribbed traditionalism will probably have taken place. So as the winter freezes come and go, a few cracks will keep occurring.

ENDNOTES

1. Other Old Regular Associations with churches in the region are the Indian Bottom Association, the Old Friendship Association, the Philadelphia Association, and the New Salem Association. The Northern New Salem Association is composed of fellowships located primarily in Ohio.

2. As reprinted in *Minutes* of the Sardis Association of Old Regular Baptists (Published by the Association, 1983), 8-9.

3. As reprinted in *Minutes* of the Sardis Association of Old Regular Baptists (Published by the Association, 1983), 8.

4. *Minutes* of the Sardis Association of Old Regular Baptists (Published by the Association, 1982), 8; and (1983), 8-9.

5. *Minutes* of the Union Association of Old Regular Baptists (Johnson City, Tenn.: Interstate Graphics, 1979), 6.

6. *Minutes* of the Sardis Association of Old Regular Baptists (Published by the Association, 1983), 9.

7. Interview with Darvin Marshall, member of the Sandy Ridge Old Regular Church, St. Paul, Virginia, December 16, 1984.

8. Interview with Mrs. Edwin May, February 15, 1985.

9. Interview with Elder Bill Campbell after service at the Bull Creek Old Regular Church, June 10, 1984.

10. Interview with one of the elders of the Bull Creek Old Regular Church, June 10, 1984.

11. Interview conducted at Bethany Old Regular Church, July 10, 1983.

12. Interview conducted in Marshall's home, July 28, 1985.

13. Interview conducted on February 15, 1985.

Appalachian Studies and the Native Student: Resource or Refuge?

by
Ricky Cox

When time came last October to submit proposals to the Appalachian Studies Conference Program Committee, I had a rough idea of what I wanted to say, but no paper, certainly no title. The one you saw printed on your progam came up at the last minute, as did the proposal itself. It serves pretty well what I want to say, but I feel I owe you all some explanation.

Originally, I had intended this to be an overview, almost a survey of native Appalachian students' reactions to, and attitudes about Appalachian Studies courses. I wrestled with this for a couple of months and found myself always faced with what I think most perceive as a problem in Appalachian studies or any study involving people. I found myself trying to classify, to group, to stereotype Appalachian students. It is difficult, and I think, unwise to attempt to identify the typical Appalachian student, just as it is hard to find that average American family with 1.8 children.

What I've finally arrived at is more of a personal view of Appalachian Studies. While I believe that some of the ideas and feelings expressed here will have meaning for some of you, I do not claim that they apply to all native students or to any except myself. With this in mind you might wish to amend the title to read: "Appalachian Studies and a Native Student: Resource or Refugee?"

I guess I should present my credentials as a native Appalachian student. I grew up in Floyd County, Virginia, about sixty miles west of Roanoke, on the eastern edge of official Appalachia, and I go to school. In my half-hearted search for the typical native student I decided that I am most definitely not this elusive person. I was twenty-six when I began attending Radford University full-time as a History major, so am subject to the condition quoted by Cratis Williams in describing Appalachian people. " ... when one chances to leave for the outside world before his personality has become set in the mold of his culture he is likely to climb far" (Williams 498). I'm afraid I've waited too long.

Maybe I am set in my ways and perhaps my perceptions and expectations of Appalachian Studies have been colored by the ambivalence demonstrated by my late arrival. I came back to school because I felt I had missed something, and that failing to return while I was able, I would one day regret it. Still, it was a struggle, giving up my job and trying to explain to my family and friends what I was doing. I suppose they thought it was a mid-life crisis twenty years early. I did finally make the commitment but not without self-doubt. Consequently, I think my involvement with Appalachian Studies has been, in part, an attempt to reconcile the two very different environments of school and work.

Now, let me tell you a little about Appalachian Studies and a native student. You may notice a few we's and our's thrown in for variety, but I have no real right to use them. I hope, though, that some of you can accept them and maybe feel a part of the I's and me's that appear far too often.

I suppose the proper way to go about answering the question posed in the title of this paper is to examine each alternative closely, weigh its relative merits, pull everything together, and then tell you in the last paragraph that I still don't have an answer. I can, however, see far enough ahead to say now that there is an answer. Appalachian Studies is both a resource and a refuge for the native student. It is a means for the native student to get around the old "apples and oranges" problem. It offers a way to compare lifestyles that revolve around two different concepts of success. I will attempt no definition of this difference, but I will offer as an example what I consider to be the most visible and painful conflict experienced by those of us who are at least exploring the possibility of seeking our fortunes in the wide world: To go or to stay?

It seems sort of senseless to spend time and money preparing yourself for a career that will never be pursued if doing so means moving beyond easy driving distance of home. I like to think that education is valuable and desirable for its own sake, but the fact remains that people expect us to "do something with" and education and that we expect the same of ourselves. We feel pressured by the mainstream notion that we must reach our fullest potential and realize our dreams if it takes marching all over Hell and half of Georgia to do it.

I listen to people at home talk and I've decided that Appalachians, at least the ones I know, don't have dreams, as such. We have "idees" or things we'd like to do if the world stands, if we live. Maybe it's setting yourself up for disappointment to say you have a dream or maybe it sounds too pretentious to say it out loud. I used to think that we come to school seeking dreams for ourselves, but perhaps we are only trying to unearth the ones we bring with us.

Jesse Stuart talks about drinking lonesome water and how it bind the mountaineer to return home (Stuart 179). It works both ways, it seems. We set out intending only to sample history, literature, philosophy and other such learned things. The tastes are strange sometimes, even bitter, but once familiar, are not easily forgotten. You would think that even the best spring water would seem pretty plain compared to heady wines. It's hard to judge.

There is a choice to be made then, and choice implies difference. I can speak with certainty only of the difference I feel each time I go home. I can't see it, so I have no color slides to show you, but I feel it and so may many of you when you read Jim Wayne Miller's "Brier Sermon" (Miller 41) or hear James Still's Lark say, "I ought ne'er thought to be a scholar" (Still 47.) With only the words of others to offer as proof, I maintain that there is a difference. To deny it is to concede that the Appalachia of the heart is a creation of the mind, a sentimental pilgrimage to places that never existed.

Appalachian Studies cannot erase the differences; it may even highlight them. It cannot make choices for young people, but hopefully it can offer a forum for more informed decision-making.

Although I've completed only two Appalachian Studies courses, I can see that there are no cut and dry approaches to the what and why of Appalachian Studies. Already, I've heard many voices saying many things about Appalachia.

The first voice I heard was Loyal Jones, telling me about Appalachian values (Jones 507). It was quite a revelation to learn that my personal quirks are shared by twenty million people. I found this piece comforting the first time I read it, and still do, but there is a burden there, waiting to fall on our shoulders. Appalachians have their own ideas about groups. We are wary of them for belonging entails responsibility for the other members. It is not required that we love or even like them, but we must look our for them, for they are ours.

This newfound identity then, is not so wonderful as it first seems for those who associate membership with responsibility. Are we bound to this group as we are a family, in which ties begin at birth and last as long as hand-me-down memories hold the threads that link names on headstones with the ones on our mailboxes? No, but there is something here that does not set well with me.

Once, I was concerned with a network of shared genes, memories, and values that haven't spread much beyond two or three counties in nearly two hundred years. Suddenly there are 397 counties and twenty million people and I just don't know if I can look after that many.

When I saw "Harlan County, U.S.A." I wanted to jump up and say, "This has nothing to do with me. These people have no connection to me. I'm not responsible for them, and I won't be made to feel guilty about de-

23

nying them. There are no coal mines where I come from, and I have no ties with them." But I do.

Last fall I had a chance to learn a little about coal mines on an Appalachian Studies field trip to the exhibition mine in Beckley, West Virginia. I was impressed, but felt no kinship with that way of life or the people who live it until I started talking to the old man who guided the tour. In following the ritual of establishing who each of us was, in terms of our respective places, I discovered that this man's father-in-law had come to West Virginia from Willis, Virginia, all of ten miles from my own home. He had been there once himself for a funeral, years ago. One of his wife's cousins had bought my Grandfather's house in Floyd. I had mistaken this man for a stranger and we were practically neighbors.

Connections exist, then, even outside the coincidental mutual acquaintance with people or places. Even if we share nothing in the way of memory or experience there is a kinship in the way we relate to new people, in the way we deal with familiar ones, and in our approach to life in general.

So we've come full circle back to Loyal Jones' list of values. To my mind his words are valid and true, as much as anything can be about such a diverse region as Appalachia. But this very fact illuminates the paradox that has evidently frustrated just about every would-be saviour of the southern mountaineer. Their validity in giving us identity as a group renders us politically ineffectual as a group, for one of our characteristics, as a group, is that we do not like groups.

Others have heard this same voice but have drawn a different meaning from the words. They, in turn, begin to speak and say, "Use these shared traits and attitudes as both foundation and mortar in building political coalitions. Band together and demand what is rightfully yours. Wake up and smell the coffee. Save Appalachia!"

Appalachia cannot be saved, at least not the one quality which makes possible all the other characteristics we point to as Appalachian. This quality is independence for ourselves and acceptance of it in others. We say that we expect others to look out for themselves and their own; it might better serve to say that we allow others to be responsible for themselves. From this precept come some of the best qualities of Appalachian people: pride, self-sufficiency, love of place, and strong sense of family. And from the same spring head flow the worst things about Appalachia: ignorance, prejudice, poverty, and exploitation of resources, both natural and human. The voices say we can change all of this and that is absolutely true. We can change all of this, not part of it. We can't sort through and pick out the pretty pieces for a quilt and make the rest into a rag rug.

Save Appalachia. Appalachia cannot be saved. We can create a new one yes, and that may be a good idea, I don't know. But the old one is dying this morning and a new one is evolving to take its place. It will live or die on its own. It will slip quietly away when it goes and no one will know until forty years later. We can all pack up and go to Washington and get things done, but we may not recognize home when we get back for it will have changed, just as we will have changed, in learning to rely on a group rather than on ourselves. Once we have acquired this civilized trait, we will be ready to live in the modern world, ready to dictate to others what is best for them, whether they know it or not. As soon as we realize our strength as a group, we can do all the things groups like to do. We can shop around for another group to feel superior to, or maybe find some people in need of cultural salvation.

If asked, I would reply to those voices, "Do as you please. Your intentions are the best, your theories are sound, and your arguments are true, but they are not of the Appalachia that I know." We talk so much about intervention and how unsympathetic it is to individual rights and concerns. When we have organized ourselves enough to eject or manipulate interventionist institutions, be they cultural, industrial, or governmental, we will ourselves have become the interventionists, and I'd rather curse someone I've never seen than the man I see in the mirror every morning.

I'm half ashamed to tell you these things. My words seem hard and callous. The humanities tell me to be a citizen of the world, to accept responsibility for my fellow man, and I find it increasingly difficult to check my attitudes at the classroom door and pick them up on the way home. They begin to seem ugly and outdated, but I am not yet ready to leave them behind. But what of Appalachian Studies? What are the voices saying? Must the native student reject individualism and fatalism to make constructive use of the insights Appalachian Studies may provide into ourselves and into our culture? I should know better than to ask, for concepts of the purpose of Appalachian Studies are as numerous as the voices that speak, the hands that write, and the minds that ponder about Appalachia. I will not ask for an answer. Instead, I will repeat the answer to my own much neglected original question. Appalachian Studies is a resource for the native student who would not carelessly trade the time-worn values of home for the shinier ideals of the larger world. It is a refuge also, for every story, every song, every triumph and every failure has some ring of the familiar, even for those like me who know nothing of coal mines or cotton mills.

I have used the idea of voices in this paper, and while it seems a bit superficial, as do all such devices, I do not think it inappropriate as ours is an oral tradition. Voices mean much to us in conversation and song. I have told you of the voices from within Appalachian Studies. I will leave you with a voice that I have yet to hear, a voice that I have wanted to hear and have listened for so intently, a voice to say, "Go home. Why worry with studying Appalachia when you can live it?"

I've waited to hear that voice and sometimes I half imagine that I do.

25

When things aren't going well I want to go home and be that fellow from Indian Valley what picks a guitar and won't drive nothing but a Ford, Carl Cox's third boy, one of Taswell Hollandsworth's grandchildren.

But I know that I never will hear that voice, and if I do I'll call the speaker a liar. I can go home, yes, and be happy there even, but I cannot go back. My people await my return and though I may see them with an altered perception, they have not changed. The road to home is still there; broken a little more by four winters, worn a little more by the wheels that roll out and back in each day, but still the same road. It is the curious traveler who has changed.

WORKS CITED

Jones, Loyal. "Appalachian Values." *Voices From the Hills*. Eds. Robert J. Higgs and Ambrose N. Manning. New York: Frederick Ungar, 1975.

Still, James. "Journey to the Forks." *The Run for the Elbertas*. Lexington: University of Kentucky Press, 1980.

Stuart, Jesse. *Beyond Dark Hills*. New York: McGraw-Hill, 1972.

Williams, Cratis. "Who Are the Southern Mountaineers?" *Voices From the Hills*. Eds. Robert J. Higgs and Ambrose N. Manning. New York: Frederick Ungar, 1975.

Dialect Effects in Appalachian Students' Written Compositions

by
Rebecca Gaeth Eller

Declining test scores over the past decade have produced a public outcry for educational reform. "Getting back to the basics" has become an oft-repeated motto, although no one has ever bothered to clearly define what is meant by "the basics." Illiteracy has been at the forefront of the controversy, and the accountability movement has generated renewed interest in grammar and phonics instruction coupled with rigorous competency testing programs.

One factor which has consistently correlated with low academic achievement has been socioeconomic status. A number of reasons for this phenomenon have been postulated, ranging from difference/deficit models to teacher and administrative bias. It has also been suggested that lower scores in language usage may be the result of "dialect interference;" i.e. because students from lower socioeconomic classes also frequently speak a non-standard dialect, their oral language may actually "interfere" with communication through formal standard English.

The extent to which certain dialects "interfere" with reading and writing standard English has been the subject of much research in recent years and has generated a great deal of controversy. Studies of language differences in reading, however, have generally failed to substantiate any dialect effects (Goodman and Buck, 1973). Research studies examining dialect influences in writing have had mixed results (Schwartz, 1982). Some researchers have found dialect-related errors in the writing of Black sixth grade youngsters to be as high as 36%, and those of Hispanic third graders to be as high as 39% (Cronnell, 1984, 1985). Other studies report some dialect influence, but have found that they have a limited effect on writing (Whiteman, 1981). Researchers who have examined the compositions of college students have found either inconsistent and weak evidence of dialect influence (Wolfram and Whiteman, 1971; Sternglass, 1974), or no significant differences between the nonstandard English usage of black and Hispanic students and their white counterparts (Kirschner and Poteet, 1973; Farr and Janda, 1985).

While there have been a number of studies which have examined dialect effects in the writing of Black and Hispanic students, few studies have been conducted which have explored dialect influences of Mountain Speech, despite the fact that Appalachian students consistently score lower on standardized tests in the area of language ability (DeYoung,

27

Vaught, and Porter, 1981). The Appalachian region has a rich oral tradition and has developed a distinct linguistic system which contains unique grammatical and phonological features (Wolfram and Christian, 1976; Wolfram, 1984). Since significant dialect effects have been found in the written compositions of elementary students from other non-mainstream populations, I was curious to see if such effects might at least partially explain the low test scores of Appalachian students. I therefore decided to explore the extent to which the features of Mountain Speech would be revealed in the compositions of youngsters from the region. I also chose to compare their writing samples to those of younsters from outside the region to determine if the two sets of compositions could be differentiated.

With the assistance of two colleagues, I obtained writing samples from two groups of sixth grade students. One group of students attends a school located in a rural mountainous county in western North Carolina, and the second attends a suburban school located near a moderately large city in central Kentucky. The youngsters were instructed to write essays on the topic of "Working Women." In order to determine which dialect features the students regularly use in their oral language, the teachers were asked to complete a lengthy dialect feature list. The written compositions were then examined for dialect influence revealed in grammatical patterns, spelling, and word choice.

The findings of the study were quite revealing. First, a mere 14% of the total surface errors of the Appalachian samples could be attributed to dialect influence. This figure is a conservative one, and in fact may over-estimatedialect-related errors. When there was a lack of subject-verb agreement, for example, this error was generally designated as being dialect-related, although admittedly this is a frequent error of all youngsters who are learning to write. Second, spelling errors accounted for 38% of the total errors in the Appalachian samples, and 30% of the errors in the non-Appalachian samples. Very few of these errors were dialect-influenced; rather, most reflected standard pronunciations which were simply misspelled. This finding supports previous research which shows that phonological differences rarely occur in writing (Whiteman, 1981). Finally, there was a lack of consistency in both the number and type of dialect-related errors. Some students had no dialect-related errors in their compositions, while others had a number of such errors. To illustrate the variation in errors, only one youngster used indirect questions (i.e. "So you say who would take over the house."), and only one student used the characteristic to + verb form ("Some people think women ought not to work."). In contrast, a number of students used "set" for "sit."

In comparing the compositions from the Appalachian and non-Appalachian students, there were obvious differences between the two groups. On the surface, the non-Appalachian samples were longer, neat-er, and contained fewer errors. The non-Appalachian students averaged 6.6 errors per sample or .27 errors per line; the Appalachian students averaged 23.6 errors per sample or 1.3 errors per line. There were also differences in style. The non-Appalachian compositions were quite formal, whereas the Appalachian compositions resembled personal narratives.

If the analysis stopped here, we might conclude that the non-Appalachian students, or at least this particular population of students, are considerably more adept at writing than the Appalachian students. Writing, however, is a form of communication. It is more than using words appropriately and placing them on the page in the proper order. Writing is a means by which we explore and transmit ideas. To focus on surface features at the expense of the ideas being conveyed neglects the true nature of written communication.

An examination of the ideas expressed in the compositions of these sixth grade youngsters again reveals substantial differences. The non-Appalachian students organized their ideas in clear paragraphs in response to specific "prompt" questions which they were asked to consider in completing the assignment. For example, in response to the question "Would it make a difference if the woman has children?," several students began the second paragraph with statements such as "If a woman has a child, it should matter." While the ideas in their compositions were certainly interesting, informative, and well-organized, there were relatively few variations in their statements.

In contrast, the compositions of the Appalachian students were more personal and individual. They were replete with vivid imagery and colorful expressions. For example, one student expressed his feelings on the subject of working women by stating that "[w]omen are not dogs or slaves for men." Another said that if women didn't work, "[t]hey would eat out of trash cans and wear rags." A male student said, "I bet women work harder than men. When women work, they work." Finally, one student expressed the real reason why women should work: "Women have to work. If they don't women will get bored and start smoking and drink coffee so bad that they will get hooked on cigarettes." In short, these compositions reflect a school environment which has capitalized on their rich oral tradition and unique culture by allowing students to express themselves freely in their own dialect.

What can we learn from the results of this research? I believe there are a number of important implications for both teachers and educational policy-makers. Before we discuss these implications, however, it is important to point out that we all speak a non-standard dialect. Every native language speaker deviates from the norms of standard English. Written language is not a direct representation of spoken language; i.e. it is not "speech written down." Speech is transient and occurs within a specific situational context. Written discourse, on the other hand, remains relatively stationary over time and functions as a standard system of communication despite variations in speech patterns. Furthermore, writing has its own special conventions. It is generally more formal than speech; it contains punctuation markers which designate particular intonation patterns; it is more highly structured and organized. Thus, while one youngster might enter school speaking a dialect which more closely resembles the written standard form than another youngster, the task for each is still the same. Both children must familiarize themselves with a more structured "literate" style, and both children must master the unique conventions of written discourse.

The findings of this study suggest that oral language variations do influence the writing of Appalachian students to a limited degree. However, dialect effects account for a relatively small number of errors. It can also be legitimately argued that the non-standard spoken dialect of all youngsters "interferes" with the writing task. Yet the Appalachian students appear to generate a proportionately greater number of surface errors in their writing than the non-Appalachian students. How can we account for these results?

I believe we must first examine how language is acquired. We do not learn language strictly by imitation, nor do we learn it by memorizing a series of rules. Rather, we learn language by using it in meaningful contexts. Written discourse is a separate "language" with its own standardized forms and conventions. The only way our students can learn the registers of written language is through exposure. We must provide ample and varied experiences with writing. We must read to them regularly at all grade levels. In short, we must immerse them in print.

Appalachian students come to school with different experiences and aspirations than those of their middle-class counterparts. Because of their working-class environment, they have had fewer experiences with written language. In many homes, books are considered a luxury, and consequently young children are not exposed to the standard English form in the critical years when their language is rapidly developing. Unless the schools provide a multitude of meaningful reading and writing experiences, these youngsters may never "catch up."

This lack of exposure to written language is reflected in the high percentage of spelling errors of both groups of students. The spelling error rate was particularly high in the compositions of the Appalachian students. Most persons erroneously assume that English is a phonetic language. Rather, it is an alphabetic language, and our spelling system is generally morphemic rather than phonetic; i.e. it tends to maintain the meaningful relationships between words at the expense of maintaining strict letter-sound relationships. (Consider, for example, *sign* and *signal*, or *medicine* and *medical*.) This system is largely learned through exposure and usage, not through memorizing a series of letter-sound correspondences, and one could rationally argue that a high number of spelling errors reflects a lack of experience with the formal printed code.

The socioeconomic conditions in the mountains may have other, less obvious effects. Since the low-skilled jobs of their parents do not require much reading and writing, many Appalachian youngsters do not see their parents modelling literacy. The economic reality of the region dictates that they, too, will probably be limited in the types of jobs they will be able to obtain. Furthermore, the values which the school is trying to impart are sometimes in direct contradicition to those of the home. It is certainly not a coincidence that the female students in the non-Appalachian region state in their compositions that they intend to become veterinarians, nurses, and office managers, whereas the female students from Appalachia believe that they will work in the local factories or become waitresses or hairdressers. Developing facility in writing cannot be very high on your list of priorities when career opportunities are simply unavailable.

Other barriers to the attainment of literacy have also been associated with low socioeconomic conditions. It has been suggested by a number of researchers that teachers are unconsciously biased against students who speak variant dialects, largely because such dialects reflect a lower-class status. In fact, although we may not wish to acknowledge that such prejudice exists, this argument has been substantiated by a considerable amount of research (Piche, Rubin, Turner, and Michlin, 1978; Rosen, 1979; Leibowicz, 1984; Ford, 1984). Joseph Leibowicz argues that "[i]f literacy is defined in such a way that students' identities and cultural norms are threatened by that definition, they will not succeed" (Leibowicz, 1984). A youngster's language is integrally related to his self-concept, and to deny his language is to deny his culture and his sense of self. When we continually imply that a child's language is "wrong," we are telling him that the language of his kinfolk and the culture which it represents are inferior. In his article entitled "The Status and Politics of Writing Instruction," Richard Hendrix states that:

> [u]ntil we can be sure that teachers have real insight into language, and into the emotional difficulty of cultural assimilation, it is hard to avoid the conclusion that minority and working class students have to go the extra mile in mastering writing... The extra effort may be justifiable in practical and social terms (many black parents now insist on it), but writing teachers at least need to acknowledge this situation, and rethink the relative weight given to different aspects of writing for the developing writer. Writing is hard enough in its own right, without becoming the arena for unacknowledged social differences (Hendrix, 1981).

31

Language is the essence of self-expression, and Appalachian students need to be able to express themselves freely, without fear of incrimination.

Unfortunately, present instructional practices may hinder, rather than promote, the attainment of literacy in Appalachia. In an overzealous attempt to raise test scores, there has been a resurgence of interest in grammar instruction. In addition, the rules of grammar are often being taught in isolation from actual writing. Not only has instruction in grammar been shown through research to be largely ineffective, but it also takes precious time away from meaningful writing experiences which provide practice in the application of standard English usage (Elley, 1976; Hillocks, 1984). As school systems become more familiar with the skills being measured on the adopted standardized tests, scores may improve for a time, but I believe that they will eventually level off and may even begin to decline if rules continue to be stressed at the expense of writing. Language simply cannot be learned outside the context of meaningful communication. We have reached the point in educational decision-making where we are allowing the tests to dictate our curriculum, rather than the needs of our students.

An overemphasis on proper grammar usage and form might also reinforce the notion of students that they "just can't write." A returned composition which has been peppered with teacher corrections can discourage even the most motivated writer. Consider the following statement of a college student from California:

> The papers you write in class—their whole attitude toward them is bad. They say the structure is not too good and the style is bad, when you are writing from your heart . . . it's like they are rejecting your whole culture (Hoover and Politzer, 1981).

When teachers focus only on surface errors and fail to acknowledge the validity of the ideas being expressed, they unconsciously communicate to students that their ideas are not important. Consequently, students "stop taking chances" and aim for proper form at the expense of generating new ideas. If we regard writing as a way of creating and organizing concepts, which I believe it is, an overemphasis on surface errors may actually stifle thinking. I am not suggesting that we ignore the writing errors of our students; I am merely suggesting that we keep them in proper perspective.

In conclusion, I would like to make several recommendations for those who are responsible for improving the writing ability of Appalachian youngsters. First, I believe it is vitally important that we build on students' strengths rather than emphasize their weaknesses. All youngsters enter school with a complex, highly developed language system. Appalachian students also have the benefit of a rich oral tradition and a distinctive heritage. Their oral language is highly expressive and colorful, and we must allow this language to shine through in their writing (Elbow, 1985). We must motivate them to write by having them communicate about things that are meaningful to them. Writing is a form of expression, and it cannot be separated from the culture which it reflects. Schools need to build upon this culture rather than reject it.

Second, it should be recognized that learning requires error. The errors in the writing of our students demonstrate transition as they struggle to master the printed code. An overemphasis on surface structure can have the detrimental effect of stifling creativity and the expression of ideas. It is important to recognize that a person can write a series of grammatical sentences, and yet have nothing to say.

Third, I believe structural elements should be taught within the context of actual writing. the conventions of written discourse can only be learned by writing, not by memorizing a grammar book. Students learn these conventions as they require them. Similarly, habitual errors can best be corrected within the context of writing by instructing students to focus on these features as they write.

Finally, I must again emphasize that it is critical that youngsters be immersed in print. Reading and writing are mutually reinforcing; both provide exposure to the formal standard code (Applebee, 1977; Kennedy, 1980; Eckhoff, 1983; Stotsky, 1983). Because of their distinct linguistic system, Appalachian students may actually require more experiences with formal written language than students from other cultures.

The Appalachian dialect is not inferior to the standard English dialect, it is simply different. In our attempt to acculturate those who remain outside the mainstream, we may be eliminating many colorful and highly expressive features of Mountain Speech. More importantly, we may be causing youngsters to reject their language and the culture associated with it. Maintaining pride in their language while developing standard written form creates a challenge for the best of teachers, but it is not an impossible task.

REFERENCES

Applebee, Arthur N. "ERIC/RCS: Writing and Reading." *Journal of Reading*, 20 (March, 1977), 534-37.

Baghban, Marcia. "The Application of Culturally Relevant Factors to Literacy Programs in Appalachia." *Reading Horizons*, 24 (Winter, 1984), 75-82.

Birnbaum, June Cannell. "Why Should I Write? Environmental Influences on Children's Views of Writing." *Theory Into Practice*, 19 (Summer, 1980), 202–210.

Cronnell, Bruce, ed. *The Writing Needs of Linguistically Different Students*. Los Alamitos, Ca.: SWRL Education Research and Development, 1981.

Cronnell, Bruce. "Dialect and Writing: A Review." *Journal of Research and Development in Education*, 17 (1983), 58–64.

Cronnell, Bruce. "Black-English Influences in the Writing of Third- and Sixth- Grade Black Students." *Journal of Educational Research*, 77 (March/April, 1984), 233–236.

Cronnell, Bruce. "Language Influences in the Writing of Third- and Sixth- Grade Mexican-American Students." *Journal of Educational Research*, 78 (Jan./Feb., 1985), 168–173.

DeYoung, Alan J.; Vaught, Charles; & Porter, Julia D. "Evaluating Educational Performance In Appalachian Kentucky." *Appalachian Journal*, 9, (Fall, 1981), 50–58.

Eckhoff, Barbara. "How Reading Affects Children's Writing." *Language Arts*, 60 (May, 1983), 607–616.

Elbow, Peter. "The Shifting Relationship Between Speech and Writing." *College Composition and Communication*, 36 (Oct., 1985), 283–303.

Elley, W.B. "The Role of Grammar in the Secondary School English Curriculum." *Research in the Teaching of English*, 10 (1976), 5–21.

Farr, Marcia and Janda, Mary Ann. "Basic Writing Students: Investigating Oral and Written Language." *Research in the Teaching of English*, 19 (February, 1985), 62–83.

Fink, Paul. *Bits of Mountain Speech*. Boone, N.C.: Appalachian Consortium Press, 1974.

Ford, Cecilia E. "The Influence of Speech Variety on Teachers' Evaluation of Students with Comparable Academic Ability." *TESOL Quarterly*, 18, (March, 1985), 25–40.

Gonzalez, Roseann Duenas. "Teaching Mexican American Students to Write: Capitalizing on the Culture." *English Journal*, 71 (November, 1982), 20–24.

Goodman, Kenneth S. & Buck, Catherine. "Dialect Barriers to Reading Comprehension Revisited." *The Reading Teacher*, 27 (October, 1973), 6–12.

Halpern, Jeanne W. "Differences Between Speaking and Writing and Their Implications for Teaching." *College Composition and Communication*, 35 (October, 1984), 345–357.

Hartwell, Patrick. "Dialect Interference in Writing: A Critical View." *Research in the Teaching of English*, 14 (May, 1980), 101–118.

Hendrix, Richard. "The Status and Politics of Writing Instruction." *Writing: The Nature, Development, and Teaching of Written Communication*. Edited by Marcia Farr Whiteman. Hillsdale, N.J.: Lawerence Erlbaum Associates, Pub., 1981.

Hillocks, George, Jr. "What Works in Teaching Composition: A Meta-analysis of Experimental Treatment Studies." *American Journal of Education*, 93 (November, 1984), 133–170.

Hoover, Mary Rhodes & Politzer, Robert L. "Bias in Composition Tests with Suggestions for a Culturally Appropriate Assessment Technique." *Writing: The Nature, Development, and Teaching of Written Communication.* Edited by Marcia Farr Whiteman. Hillsdale, N.J.: Lawrence Erlbaum Associates, Pub., 1981.

Kennedy, Mary Lynch. "Reading and Writing: Interrelated Skills of Literacy on the College Level." *Reading World*, 20 (December, 1980), 131-141.

Kirschner, S.A., & Poteet, G.H. "Non-Standard English Usage in the Writing of Black, White, and Hispanic Remedial English Students in An Urban Community College." *Research in the Teaching of English*, 7 (Winter 1973), 351-355.

Leibowicz, Joseph. "ERIC/RCS Report: Classrooms, Teachers, and Nonstandard Speakers." *Language Arts*, 61 (January, 1984), 188-191.

Lipscomb, Delores H. "Perspectives on Dialects in Black Students' Writing." *Curriculum Review*, 17 (August, 1978), 167-169.

Meier, Terry Ryan, & Cazden, Courtney B. "Research Update: A Focus on Oral Language and Writing from a Multicultural Perspective." *Language Arts*, 59 (May, 1982), 504-512.

Piche, Gene L.; Rubin, Donald L.; Turner, Lona J.; & Michlin, Michael L. "Teachers' Subjective Evaluations of Standard and Black Nonstandard English Compositions: A Study of Written Language and Attitudes." *Research in the Teaching of English*, 12 (May, 1978), 107-118.

Porter, Julia Damron. "Appalachia: Adrift in the Mainstream." *Theory Into Practice*, 20 (Winter, 1981), 13-19.

Rosen, Lois. "An Interview with William Labov." *English Journal*, 68 (March, 1979), 16-19.

Schwartz, Judith I. "Dialect Interference in the Attainment of Literacy." *Journal of Reading*, (February, 1982), 440-446.

Sternglass, M.A. "Close Similarities in Dialect Features of Black and White College Students in Remedial Composition Classes." *TESOL Quarterly*, 8, (September, 1974), 271-283.

Stotsky, Sandra. "Research on Reading/Writing Relationships: A Synthesis and Suggested Directions." *Language Arts*, 60 (May, 1983), 627-642.

Stubbs, Michael. *Language and Literacy: The Sociolinguistics of Reading and Writing.* Boston: Routledge & Kegan Paul Ltd., 1980.

Whiteman, Marcia Farr. "Dialect Influence in Writing." *Writing: The Nature, Development, and Teaching of Written Communication.* Edited by Marcia Farr Whiteman. Hillsdale, N.J.: Lawrence Erlbaum Associates, Pub., 1981.

Wolfram, Walt, & Whiteman, Marcia. "The Role of Dialect Interference in Composition." *The Florida FL Reporter*, 9 (Spring/Fall, 1971), 34-38, 59.

Wolfram, Walt, & Christian, Donna. *Appalachian Speech.* Arlington, Va.: Center for Applied Linguistics, 1976.

Wolfram, Walt. "Language Assessment in Appalachia: A Sociolinguistic Perspective." *Appalachian Journal*, 4, (Spring/Summer, 1977), 224–234.

Wolfram, Walt. "Is There an 'Appalachian English'?" *Appalachian Journal*, 11 (Spring, 1984), 215–224.

Old Catawbans and "Mountain Grill": The Appalachian in Thomas Wolfe's Short Stories

by
Sally Bruce

They have been described as hillbillies, hicks and backwoods clod-hoppers. Even before the turn of the century, the people of the southern Appalachians were singled out as "different." Different in their speech, in their way of living, in their outlook and in their customs. Those that visited the region capitalized on this difference. Writers such as Mary Murfree and John Fox, Jr. described the quaint way of speaking and curiously rural way of life to the rest of the country. By the early 1920's, even those from the area saw the backwoods mountain people as different, different even from their neighbors in the cities. One of these people was Thomas Wolfe. Beginning with folk plays during his years at Chapel Hill and Harvard and continuing through his final project, "The Hills Beyond," Wolfe describes in eloquent and poetic language the people from his native mountains. Drawing on folklore and regional history told to him by his mother and her people in the Swannanoa Valley, Wolfe paints the picture of another kind of Old Catawban. Although not above relating the tall tales and worst side or "mountain grill" of the Appalachians, Wolfe does not single out the mountaineer for particular scorn. Indeed, his portraits of Boston and New York are just as scathing. Influenced by the stories and writers of the period, his own relatives and related from a viewpoint which was half northern, Wolfe's Appalachian is an intelligent, resourceful, industrious, backwoodsman who represented not only his own mountains, but indeed the entire fabric of America.

Although Wolfe was born in a town of fifteen thousand, many considered his own "larger than life" character to be typically mountaineer. In 1937, he wrote F. Scott Fitzgerald:

> "The Little fellows who don't know may picture a man as a great exuberant six foot six clodhopper straight out of nature who bites off half a plug of apple tobacco, tilts the liquor jug and lets half of it gurgle down his throat, wipes off his mouth with the back of one hairy paw, jumps three feet in the air and clacks his heels together four times before he hits the floor again and yells "Whoopee boys, I'm a roarin', tootin', shootin', son of a gun from Buncombe County - out of my way now, here I come!."..[1]

37

In fact, Wolfe's own background was far from the backwoods. The Asheville Wolfe was born in what was already a cosmopolitan town undergoing a real estate boom which drew people from all across the country. He spent half his life in Boston and New York City and, as he wrote his mother in 1923; "I have stepped on toes right and left - I spared Boston with its nigger sentimentalists no more than the South which I love but which I am nevertheless pounding."[2]

Indeed, Wolfe's heritage was only half southern, as his father was from York Springs, Pennsylvania. In 1933, Wolfe wrote a boyhood friend:

> ... I have had that feeling of familiarity and home only in two places. One is the country where I was born, western North Carolina, and the other is my father's country, among the farms and orchards of the Pennsylvania Dutch in southern Pennsylvania.[3]

Wolfe's objective point of view toward mountaineer culture came in part from his father's side of the family. That was not to say that W.O. Wolfe was an objective observer of mountain people. It was W.O., after all, who originated the term "mountain grill" as a derogatory stereotype of his own creation. In later years, when Mrs. Wolfe was asked where her husband had obtained the phrase, she replied; "I guess he made it up. A mountain grill must be somebody that is ignorant; not much above an animal. East Tennessee mountain grill. ... If he wanted to make anybody mad he would say, 'Nothing but a mountain grill.' "[4] Nevertheless, that northern outlook from his father and from his years at Harvard and New York provided Wolfe with an identity separate from the mountains which allowed him to step back and see the area more objectively than would otherwise have been possible.

Wolfe was also influenced to some extent by local color writers of the era. His first encounters with literature came from his father's library, now part of the Thomas Wolfe Memorial, Wolfe's boyhood home in Asheville. W.O. Wolfe's books range from Balzac to Stevenson and include many of the early local color writers such as Washington Irving and Brett Hart, which reflect Wolfe's own descriptions. One of these became an example for Wolfe of what he did not want his own work to become. In 1923, he wrote his mother from Harvard about a play he was working on:

> The point to this play, mama, grows out of my indignation at the idea most people have of mountain life, growing out of the romantic stories of mountain life by such writers as John Fox, Jr. and others. You and I know this is not the truth.[5]

Despite these protests, however, Wolfe's early work incorporated many of the same stereotypical elements he disdained. He adopted a different kind of stereotype from James Boyd, author of Drums and Marching On. According to Wolfe's friend, Jonathon Daniels, Wolfe was tremendously impressed by Boyd; particularly in his sentiments toward the piedmont, that "flat lands make a flat and colorless people."[6] It was this belief that led Wolfe time and time again back to his own roots in the southern Appalachians. Though influenced by other writers, Wolfe's prose was uniquely his own.

It was the influence of his mother's people from the Swannanoa Valley just east of Asheville that Wolfe gained the inspiration for his short stories on the area. Julia Westall was born a year before the Civil War to a family of eleven children. Her father, Thomas Casey Westall, was a farmer, surveyor, teacher, carpenter and major in the North Carolina militia. He married his first cousin, Martha Penland, who was a great-granddaughter of Robert Patton, one of the first settlers in the area. It was through the Patton connection, too, that Wolfe was related to Davey Crockett, who married a Patton girl.[7] After the Civil War, the family moved farther up the Swannanoa Valley to a hundred acre farm and it was the stories from this mountainous tract that Mrs. Wolfe passed on to her youngest son. Wolfe inherited not only his storytelling ability but also his remarkable memory from his mother and grandfather. As Mrs. Wolfe recalled; "Father was a very fine man. None of his children took after him. Tom was the only one that took after him in writing. Tom was named after him. None of his children measured up to him."[8] Although some of the Westalls moved to Asheville, many continued to live in the hills, giving Wolfe an excellent first person account of some of the rich background and heritage of his ancestors.

Wolfe's original plan for the material dealing with his Appalachian forebears was to create a novel, orginally entitled The Hills Beyond Pentland. This book would trace the history of Eugene Gant, the hero in Wolfe's first two novels, Look Homeward, Angel and Of Time and the River, back to the 1830's and his grandfather's day. Wolfe also had plans for three more novels which would further chronicle the Gant and Pentland families and ultimately depict American life from colonial days, with the arrival of the first Pentland to America, to the Depression of the 1930's and Wolfe's own career as a novelist.[9] Although he ended up abandoning his plans for the three intervening novels, The Hills Beyond was still at the back of his mind even as he worked on his manuscript for The Web and the Rock. When finally published after Wolfe's death in 1938, the book contained many portions of the Pentland family saga in its first half. As early as 1934, Wolfe added in a postscript to his mother a request for information on the older branches of her family to provide a background for his project.

... if I tell how one family like your own, for instance, going back a hundred and fifty years or more to pioneer and Colonial days and with all their settling in various places, pushing Westward marrying into other families everywhere, etc., finally weaving a kind of web, it would have the whole history of the country in it. [10]

When he began working on the project in earnest, however, he found that much of the material had already been published in the form of short stories and other novels and he was forced to begin once more from scratch. He changed the name from Pentland to Joyner and the fragment, called "The Hills Beyond," was eventlually included in a book of short stories by that name after his death. Several other short stories in this collection contain portrayals of mountain life as described by Wolfe, including "Chickamauga" and "The Return of the Prodigal." Two other short stories based on Appalachian life appear in his first collection of short stories, From Death to Morning; "The Web of Earth" and "The Men of Old Catawba." In each, Wolfe puts his own observations of the mountain people which still provide valuable insights into Appalachian culture.

The first of Wolfe's short stories to deal with his mother and her family was entitled "The Web of Earth," published in the spring of 1932. It originated from a conservation he had with his mother in January of that year when she visited him in New York. Mrs. Wolfe's long, rambling narrative is an excellent example of Wolfe's mastery of dialect, for the entire ninety page story consists of the rememberances of Eliza Gant from her childhood during the Civil War to her husband's previous marriages and the birth of her children:

> I reckon that they tried to put it down in books, all of the wars and battles. Child, I guess they got that part of it all right, but Lord! - how could these fellows know the way it was when they weren't born, when they weren't there to see it; they made it seem so long ago and like it happened in some strange land - what could they know, child, of the way it was.... [11]

"The Web of Earth" portrays Eliza Gant as a type of "earth mother" and her husband as the "far wanderer." [12] Through Wolfe's skillful weaving of many different story lines, she evolves from a rather confused, misplaced mountaineer to a woman in full possession of her faculties, anxious to impart to her son some of the vivid memories and stories in their family history. And in fact, nearly all aspects of that family history are touched upon in the narrative. Wolfe wrote his mother in May of 1932:

40

The story is about everything that goes to make up life—the happiness, the sorrow, the joy, the pain, the triumph, and the suffering.... As for the person who tells the story, everything that is written is written as an honorable tribute to her courage, strength, and character.[13]

Many critics, including Wolfe's editor Maxwell Perkins and literary agent Elizabeth Nowell, consider "The Web of Earth" to be one of Wolfe's best works.[14] His style of writing is particularly suited to this "stream of consciousness" prose; the piece was one of the few which Perkins returned to Wolfe with the comment, "Not one word of this should be changed."[15]

"The Men of Old Catawba" did not receive the same critical acclaim as "The Web of Earth." Indeed, it appears to be very much a forgotten story, included in the same short story collection as "The Web of Earth" and essentially ignored thereafter. Wolfe did not forget the story, however. Although orginally written in 1935, Wolfe drew on the same descriptions for the opening of "The Hills Beyond" as he did for "The Men of Old Catawba": "On the middle-Atlantic seaboard of the North American continent and about a day's journey from New York, is situated the American State of Old Catawba."[16] In "The Hills Beyond," this became: "About midway along the Atlantic Seaboard of the North American continent lies a strip of land which is known today as the state of Old Catawba."[17] Where "The Hills Beyond" goes into the story of the Lost Colony, however, "The Men of Old Catawba" relates the story of the discovery of Old Catawba through a one-eyed Spaniard and his quest for gold. The story was originally written as two separate tales, one called "Polyphemus" and the other "Old Catawba." It was incorporated into one when included in From Death to Morning. Wolfe is attempting to set the stage for his Appalachian characters in these stories and they prove the admiration Wolfe held for the people of his native state:

> Their character has strong Scotch markings: they are cautious and deliberate, slow to make a radical decision. They are great talkers, and believe in prayer and argument. They are perhaps the most immensely conservative people on earth, they reverence authority, tradition, and leadership, but when committed to any decision, they stick to it implacably.[18]

At least one of the stories in this essay came from a professor at Chapel Hill. When Wolfe himself was teaching at Washington Square College in New York University, he had his students read books, like Glenway Westcott's The Grandmothers, which dealt with the same material

41

Wolfe had always planned to work on in his own novels.[19] The character analysis was Wolfe's own, however, and his insightful descriptions into the mountaineer psyche are in many ways applicable even today.

"The Return of the Prodigal" was a deviation from Wolfe's Hills Beyond Pentland, but it nevertheless presents some interesting insights into Wolfe's view of Appalachian culture. The first part of the story, "The Thing Imagined" was written in 1934 when Asheville's reception of Look Homeward, Angel was still fresh in Wolfe's mind. It relates an imaginary trip back to his hometown in which even his own mother does not recognize him but receives him as just another roomer in her boardinghouse. The second half, written after Wolfe's actual visit home in 1937, proves that the people of Asheville had actually forgiven him, though it took nearly seven years for them to arrive at that point. Wolfe came home by way of Burnsville, just north of Asheville, where he met many of his mother's relatives still living in the area:

> Yore grandpaw, son, was my own brother. He was born, like all of us, on the South Toe in Zebulon. He married yore grandmaw thar and settled down and raised a family. His paw before him - my paw, too - he come in thar long years before. I've heerd him tell it was wild country then. Thar was Cherokees when yore great-grandpaw first come in thar. Yes, sir.[20]

Wolfe's account of this stopover in Burnsville is full of warmth and humor, quite a different attitude from the bitter one which raised the wrath of his hometown in his first novel. Even an account of a brutal shooting in the streets of downtown Burnsville is interpersed with humor as the murderer turns to "Eugene" and says:

> "Who's this?"
> "Must be a cousin of yours, Ted. Leastways, he's a cousin of mine. You know - the feller who wrote that book."
> With a slow and sullen grin Ted shifts the gun and offers his hand.
> "Why, sure, I know about you. I know your folks. But, by God, you'd better never put this in a book! Because if you do - " with a shake of the head and a throaty laugh - "you and me's goin' to get together!"[21]

In real life, Wolfe actually was a witness to an encounter between the two men he wrote about, if not the actual murder, and was called back from New York to give testimony at their trial.[22] The whole affair had a deep effect on Wolfe, who felt the murder had taken place in part because of the men's wish to become part of one of Wolfe's novels. They did. Wolfe wrote about the encounter not only in "The Return of the Prodigal," it was also incorporated into his last novel, You Can't Go Home Again.

The trip home in 1937 also provide Wolfe with the source for another story, "Chickamauga." While in Burnsville, he spoke in length with his ninety-five year old great-uncle John Westall, who remembered the Civil War battle in great detail. Wolfe later spoke quite warmly of Uncle John to his editor, Edward Aswell, and said that "the old man told his story in almost exactly the words in which it appears....."[23]

> We never knowed how hit would be there in the cedar thickets beside Chickamauga Creek. And if we had a-knowed, if someone ha a-told us, why I reckon that none of us would a-cared. And as fer knowin' - law! The only trouble about knowin' is that you've got to know what knowin's like before you know what knowin' is. Thar's no one can tell you.[24]

Through his use of folk speech to tell the story of the battle, Wolfe's "Chickamauga" has veen called "one of the most effective representations of mountaineer speech in American literature."[25] The story is effective more for this reason that because it gives an accurate account of the battle. By telling it from the perspective of Uncle John, Wolfe did not need to be concerned with historical accuracy, for the story does have many discrepancies when compared to the actual battle. Wolfe drew on his own imagination as well as the recollections of his great-uncle and his own reading of history; whether or not there was actually cedar thicket at the Battle of Chickamauga becomes immaterial, the fact that Uncle John remembers it is not. Critics of the time were not enamored of Wolfe's story. Though he sent it to a dozen different magazines, trying to earn some pocket money between novels, each rejected it in turn until in desperation he finally sent it to the Yale Review. The Review paid him just enough to buy a good overcoat, which was badly needed.[26] Other pieces did better in magazines and, in all, Wolfe published nearly sixty pieces of fiction in various magazines, from Redbook to The New Republic, emphasizing his wide appeal to the reading public.

Perhaps the most important of Wolfe's accounts of mountain life come in the form of a fragment from the piece he was working on right before his death in 1938. Dropping the name Pentland to separate the work from his previous novels, Wolfe called it "The Hills Beyond." It traces the Joyner family back to the 1970's with their first settling in Zebulon County, North Carolina. This has been called Wolfe's most objective work; the characters, with one or two exceptions, are fictional. He had moved away from the romanticism that marked his early efforts to a realistic account of frontier life. He recounts not only the story of the Joyner family, but also many legends and tall tales that marked frontier life, making his work valuable as folklore as well as regional history. The story begins with William "Bear" Joyner and his family; seven children by the first marriage, sixteen by the second; a character based on Wolfe's own great-grandfather. Bear is also a likenss to a man found in another family tree; that of Zebulon Vance, North Caroina's Civil War govenor. In fact, many similarities can be drawn between the two families, a fact which was not lost on Wolfe. Zachariah Joyner, one of Bear's sons, is based on Vance. In fact, Wolfe claims to have collected "more than eight hundred stories, anecdotes, and jokes that are told of him, and of this number at least six hundred have the unmistakable ring—or smack—of truth. If they did not happen—they should have!"[27] He goes on to relate many of these tales; Vance's backwoods humor was legendary even among the people of his homeland, such as the tale in which he assures the U.S. Senate that he "could—halfway across the stream" and the Vice President declares him out of order. "Mr. President, sir, you are right," declares the Senator; "If I was in order, sir, I could—the whole way across it!"[28] Legendary feats are also the basis of Wolfe's description of Bear Joyner, a fact which Wolfe puts into perspective from the first:

> Bear Joyner, like his famous son, was increate with myth, because the very nature of the man persuaded it.... The Myth is founded on extorted fact: wrenched from the context of ten thousand days, and rutted roads, the desolations of lost voices long ago.... It is important then to know that William Joyner "chewed the b'ar." But it is even more important to know that William Joyner was a man who learned to read a book.[29]

Wolfe's mountaineer in "The Hills Beyond" is not a slow, ignorant farmer as some had portrayed him. He was instead a strong, industrious, intelligent man who incorporated many of the traits of Americans as a whole. Indeed, several of the sons of Bear leave the rural mountain life for professions in the city, including Lafayette, the grandfather of George Webber, Wolfe's hero in The Web and the Rock and You Can't Go Home Again. Had he been able to finish the novel, the storyline would have taken the family to the opening of The Web and The Rock. As it is, it brings the story through the generations of the Joyner family up to 1880, or twenty years before George's birth. Thus it is only a fragment of the intended novel, but it is an important one to his development as a writer and his perception of the mountaineer stereotype.

Thomas Wolfe's short stories depict a mountain people as diverse as the country they settled in. From the rambling reminscences of Eliza Gant and Uncle John Pentland, to the violence and threats of a local murderer, the political oratory of Zachariah Joyner, and the legends and tall tales of the men of Old Catawba and Bear Joyner, Wolfe's stories cannot be said to fit any one stereotype. His characters are neither all "good Old Catawbans" nor all "mountain grill." They would instead settle in all parts of the country, founding families in Boston, Massachusetts and Seattle, Washington as well as Asheville, North Carolina. Wolfe's northern heritage, his wide readings of other authors, and his extensive travels abroad gave his mountaineer a universal appeal which made him just as popular in Germany as in the United States. His plan was to tell the story of the whole country through her people; a massive job which Wolfe's short twelve year career as a novelist did not allow him to complete. That which was completed provided an overwhelming body of work with all of the sights and sounds which Wolfe absorbed over the years. His powers of observation were so renowned that the science fiction writer Ray Bradbury based his short story "Forever and the Earth" on him. The story brings Wolfe back to life in the year 2257 to describe an interplanetary journey to which only Wolfe could do justice. His descriptions of space, as his descriptions of Appalachia, are based on a viewpoint which is at once objective yet filled with warmth and insight that marked so much of his later works. Wolfe's descriptions are timeless and his writing, whether on his home mountains or on outer space, are universal.

ENDNOTES

1. Elizabeth Nowell, editor, *The Letters of Thomas Wolfe* (New York: Charles Scribner's Sons, 1956), p. 644.

2. C. Hugh Holman and Sue Fields Ross, editors, *The Letters of Thomas Wolfe to his Mother* (Chapel Hill: The University of North Carolina Press, 1968), p. 42.

3. Nowell, p. 376.

4. Hayden Norwood, *The Marble Man's Wife* (New York: Charles Scribner's Sons, 1947), p. 76.

5. Holman and Fields, p. 17.

6. Jonathon Daniels, "Poet of the Bloom," *Tar Heels* (Dodd Mead & Co, 1941).

7. James Meehan, "Thomas Wolfe as Regional Historian," *The Thomas Wolfe Review*, Volume 1, Number 1, Spring 1977, p. 9.

8. Norwood, p. 46.

9. Richard S. Kennedy, *The Window of Memory* (Chapel Hill: The University of North Carolina Press, 1962), p. 199-200.

10. Holman and Fields, p. 234.

11. Thomas Wolfe, "The Web of Earth," *From Death to Morning* (New York: Charles Scribner's Sons, 1970), p. 214-215.

12. Kennedy, p. 242.

13. Holman and Fields, p. 220-221.

14. Bruce R. McElderry, Jr., *Thomas Wolfe* (New York: Twayne Publishers, Inc., 1964), p. 111.

15. Kennedy, p. 243.

16. Thomas Wolfe, "The Men of Old Catawba, *From Death to Morning* (New York: Charles Scribner's Sons, 1970), p. 185.

17. Thomas Wolfe, "The Hills Beyond," *The Hills Beyond* (New York: The New American Library, 1982), p. 157.

18. Thomas Wolfe, "The Men of Old Catawba, *From Death to Morning* (New York: Charles Scribner's Sons, 1970), p. 201.

19. Kennedy, p. 241.

20. Thomas Wolfe, The Return of the Prodigal," *The Hills Beyond* (New York: The New American Library, 1982), p. 49.

21. Ibid., p. 103.

22. Floyd C. Watkins, *Thomas Wolfe's Characters* (Norman: The University of Oklahoma Press, 1957), p. 134-135.

23. Edward C. Aswell, "A Note on Thomas Wolfe," *The Hills Beyond* (New York: The New American Library, 1982), p. 297.

24. Thomas Wolfe, "Chickamauga," *The Hills Beyond* (New York: The New American Library, 1982), p. 78.

25. Floyd C. Watkins, "Rhetoric in Southern Writing," *Georgia Quarterly*, XIII, Spring 1958.

26. Aswell, p. 298.

27. Thomas Wolfe, "The Hills Beyond," *The Hills Beyond* (New York: The New American Library, 1982), p. 174.

28. Ibid., p. 174.

29. Ibid., p. 169-170.

BIBLIOGRAPHY

Primary Sources

Holman, Hugh C. and Ross, Sue Fields, ed. *The Letters of Thomas Wolfe to his Mother*. Chapel Hill, The University of North Carolina Press, 1968.

Nowell, Elizabeth, ed. *The Letters of Thomas Wolfe*. New York, Charles Scribner's Sons, 1956.

Wolfe, Thomas. *From Death to Morning*. New York, Charles Scribner's Sons, 1970.

Wolfe, Thomas. *The Hills Beyond*. New York, New American Library, 1982.

Secondary Sources

Aswell, Edward C. "A Note on Thomas Wolfe," *The Hills Beyond*. New York, New American Library, 1982.

Daniels, Jonathon. "Poet of the Bloom," *Tar Heels*. Dodd, Mead and Company, 1941.

Field, Leslie A. "The Hills Beyond: A Folk Novel of America," *Three Decades of Criticism*. New York, New York Univeristy Press, 1968

Geismar, Maxwell. "Thomas Wolfe: The Hillman and the Furies," *Yale Review*, 1946.

Higgs, Robert J. and Manning, Ambrose N., ed. *Voices from the Hills*. New York, Frederick Ungar Publishing, 1975.

Holman, Hugh C. *The Loneliness at the Core*. Baton Rouge, Louisiana State University Press, 1975.

Kennedy, Richard S. "Thomas Wolfe and the American Experience," *Modern Fiction Studies*. Purdue University, Volume XI, Number 3.

Kennedy, Richard S. *The Window of Memory*. Chapel Hill, The University of North Carolina Press, 1962.

McElderry, Bruce R. *Thomas Wolfe*. New York, Twayne Publishers, 1964.

Meehan, James. "Thomas Wolfe as Regional Historian," *The Thomas Wolfe Newsletter*. Volume 1, Number 1, Spring 1977.

Muller, Herbert J. *Thomas Wolfe*. New York, Vail-Ballow Press, 1947.

Norwood, Hayden. *The Marble Man's Wife*. New York, Charles Scribner's Sons, 1947.

Perkins, Maxwell. "Thomas Wolfe," *Harvard Library Bulletin*. Autumn, 1947.

Walser, Richard. "Major Thomas Casey Westhall," *The Thomas Wolfe Review*. Volume 8, Number 2, Fall 1984.

Walser, Richard. *Thomas Wolfe: An Introduction and Interpretation*. New York, Barnes and Noble, Inc., 1961.

Watkins, Floyd C. "Rhetoric in Southern Writing," *Georgia Review*. Volume XII, Spring 1958.

Watkins, Floyd C. *Thomas Wolfe's Characters*. Norman, University of Oklahoma Press, 1957.

Appalachian Crafts As Literary Subject

by
Bennie Sinclair

As a contemporary writer I have found our Appalachian handcrafts to be a challenging subject for poetry and fiction. The language and work ethic of crafts, as well as the craftspeople and their produce, offer stimulating ground for the creative writer. The crafts of pottery, spinning, and weaving are represented here in poems and novella excerpts.

Nowhere in the New World has the pervasion of handcrafts been greater than in the Southern Appalachians. Forests yielded logs for carving and lumber for furniture as well as bark, berries, and plants for dyeing and "woods pretties," baskets and brooms. The earth gave clay and gemstones. Hillside pastures nourished sheep whose coats were a harvest, and fields grew cotton that likewise could be transformed into the miracle of fiber.

Isolation made it easy for highlanders to be self-sufficient. Idle hands were a sin, busy hands were a virtue. "Use it up wear it out; make it do or do without" led to thrifty and clever use of usable objects designed to be attractive and inexpensive. With all or many stages of the production done by hand, the work ethic became as important as the work itself.

As a child I was surrounded by crafts still in use in our home, from dough bowl to quilts, and, though stilled, my great-grandmother's spinning wheel was a reminder of how the woven coverlets in our linen closet had begun as thread. All of my adult life I've been closely involved with the crafts field through my husband, Don Lewis, and his work as a potter and member of the Southern Highland Handicraft Guild. An awareness of how the past continues into the present in the area of crafts, and a con-

49

stant re-evaluation of that relationship by the craftsperson comparing old ways and new, old values and new, is to me symbolic of the writer's dilemma as well.

The Apprentice

I live in the potter's house,
a house transformed of clay;
of tools, dust, machinery; mounds
that wait in vinegary stillness,
for their metamorphic day.

Of the potter's hand
I take myself transformed
into each shaping hour, an humbled,
hopeful witness
to the miracle of clay

made whole
by that most destructive of elements, fire;
or coming ever back into itself wet down,
dried out, wet down again; pounded, thrown
on the potter's wheel

into shapes both basic and fine, coming
of purpose at last from the potter's
magnificent hand while I, the novitiate,
cannot come so close of the clay
can only pretend

to sense its lifelike resiliency
as I carry unpromising mounds
from the bins to his wheel. On glazing day
I stand in the muck of chemicals
and watch the potter select

for each a piece of skin: considering, for a cup,
how its rim will feel upon lips
or, if a bowl, how its texture might seem
to a woman's sensitive hands. Each form
that the potter makes

becomes, as himself, an image reflected.
Through his miscalculations I learn
that this work leaves nothing to chance;
the smallest detail of design
has bearing over the whole—

the pitcher not fully thought out
will never pour cleanly;
the lid less carefully turned
will ruin the effect of a jar. From the moment
his process begins

through the final stages of the kiln
the potter gives life, or destroys,
of his worth. Myself,
I have yet to be judged. Seven years
in the potter's house

shall teach me technical skill: but whatever
I make of my clay will depend; will depend.

I was deeply moved when I first saw Doris Ulmann's photograph,
"A Spinner In Her Hundredth Year." In it, it seemed that continuity existed not so much in the craft of spinning and weaving as in this particular craftswoman's longevity, which transcended generations. When I began research I was struck by the poetic possiblities of the language related to these skills especially pattern names.

"A Spinner In Her Hundredth Year"
from the photograph by Doris Ulmann

Once, she herded colors like sheep
from off the hillsides,
perfecting the dyeing science
that all hues of light
and shadow might hold fast—
a greater span
she learned to reason in.

In spring, she envisioned the little lambs
grown coats like Joseph's—
matched eyes the deepness of sky
to indigo;
their blood to madder.

51

In and out of our time
her low or high
wheels flew, their miles
concentric.

Whenever the spindle was stilled
threads and yarn she had drawn
carried her through the night
like a wind-blown spider—
adrift in years, as seasons,
each coming round again.

Children, grandchildren,
great great grandchildren...
so many times she witnessed
color and cloth of her hand
in and out of the church;
the tomb or the marriage bed;
she came to remember
only the names of the thread,
or their design.

Mornings, she ran the sheep from their stalls
into the high pasture:
evenings, she gathered them in,
calling them by their names;
watching the spread of her patterns
fashion itself to their skins:
 Rose
 in the Garden
 Rose
 in the Blossom
 Rose
 in the Wilderness:
and each spring, a dozen new lambs;
skeins running now on the mountain.

My novella *The Loom House* follows a young weaver's career through
the crafts revival of the 1960's through the 1970's. During this period
Trudy sees crafts re-identified as "art," and the integral dictum "produce
or perish" altered by creation of the National Endowment for the Arts
and accompanying states arts agencies which award grants money to
those educated and industrious in seeking it. She sees, in her own field,
the painstaking learning of a skill confused with instant interpretation of

the medium. She finds a moral dilemma in being a modern craftsperson. Should she spend time refining her art and seeking out markets . . . or in filling out grant applications and cultivating contacts? Is it demeaning to pay to submit her work to exhibits? In seeking answers she becomes a scholar of the past as well as the present world of weaving. Following are three excerpts.

Three excerpts from *The Loom House*:

. . . And, as if to prove it, she stood up, stretched, and went into her studio. But the sudden colors of her yarns, pinned close to the rafters on closeline, touched her with the same effect, of memories.

"Well, then, I guess I'd better get going," Ola said, from the doorway. "It's a long way back to civilization. I'd feel so much better if you had a phone . . ."

Trudy waved goodbye. She listened to the Mercury slough its way through the mud to the paved road and then, sighing, reached up and plucked a skein of gray wool from the line, holding it to her face like a flower. In the dyepot it had stunk of sumac and the copperas she used as a mordant, but now it was cleaned and fresh, waiting for the loom. Before this depressing period of lethargy had set in, in which she could get nothing done, she had spent weeks at dyeing, working toward certain hues that haunted her, though she had no idea how she would use them. On clear days she had foraged her woods and fields for dyestuffs. Her basketfuls of weeds and flowers and leaves, roots and lichens and barks filled the cabin's old rooms with fresh pungency.

And slowly out of the dyepot strange and true colors had begun to bloom: sombre and rich reds of sassafras and dogwood root; a vibrant, painfully youthful green of oak leaves crushed and pounded, the color held fast by salting; mournful purples and blues from a half-dozen or more different berry plants; and one special shade that almost eluded her, a glowing and elegant brown that she thought must be the same richness of her late mother's hair. That brown had come, finally, of walnut gathered after frost, a mixture of hulls, roots and bark, tended and stirred to an exact moment. It had seemed particulary fitting that this shade needed no mordant to "sadden" it or make it hold true, as it did in Trudy's mind.

"Mother's Hair," "Finch's Wing"—it was her habit to give names to her colors, once she had achieved them. The un-named gray in her hand was as soft and indistinct as fog, or the mists that rolled from the hills each morning. It was so subtle it would be difficult to work with, she knew. And, against her will, she saw the gray as something else . . ." Childhood?" That hazy period of first becoming aware of that tragedy being played out around her?

During her first years, the war years, it had seemed so strange, as if there was a cadence in the air that everyone seemed to hear—a roll of drums and a sound of taps, the rumble of convoys passing in the night. It seemed a different world then, something to do with camaraderie; unspoken feelings somehow shared. Often she had stood on the sidewalk to wave at the military traffic moving to and from the air base just outside of town. In a newsreel, when she saw a thin, tow-haired little girl waving at truckloads of soldiers, she cried out loud, in amazement, "That's *me!*"

"No, dear, that's a little girl in England," her mother whispered, and around them, in the darkened theatre, everyone laughed good-naturedly.

... Her father, Hamp, felt sorry for himself. In the throes of self-pity drank and stayed home from work. Growing suddenly sentimental, he decided to take Trudy on a pilgrimage to her mother's homeplace, where the child's great-grandmother, whom he always referred to as "the crone," still lived.

It was the first time since leaving the hospital that Trudy had felt truly awake. They rode for hours in the afternoon, stopping in some small foothills town for supper. As it began to turn dark the road became narrow; mountainous; frightening. Trudy lay under a blanket in the back seat and closed her eyes, terrified—but when she woke she was in a bed, and the sky was lightening. Her gnarled and tiny great-grandmother bent over her like some creature remembered from a dream, shushing her to be quiet, pointing warningly across the room where Hamp lay snoring.

Conspiratorially the old woman led her into the warm kitchen, helped her dress, and fed her a steaming breakfast. Then, her watery eyes eager as the child's she took Trudy on a tour of the homeplace that, amid morning mist and bird music, again seemed familiar, like a dream. Perhaps her mother had described it to her, or there had been pictures. There was the cluster of old log buildings, the waking cackle of hens, the cow. Tools lay in the high grass, abandoned and rusting; the barn and smokehouse were rotting from leaky roofs.

Clutching her heavy skirt up about her knobby knees, the old woman led the way slowly through the morning damp while Trudy limped as slowly behind, falling instantly in love with each and everything she saw. They visited the hens and cow, the deserted buildings where kittens spilled from the rafters like mice. Then her great-grandmother unlocked the door to the loom house and led Trudy in. Two great looms stood idle, one strung and abandoned in the middle stages of a coverlet now ghostly gray with dust. Yet, despite the disarray, the sight of those threads in their paradigm captured Trudy's imagination. As instinctively as a young spider coming into her own first web, Trudy responded to the compelling pull of thread and loom.

...Now, standing alone and somewhat afraid in her studio twenty years later, Trudy recognized the colors around her, that she had been creating. In a moment of unexpected understanding, Ola had once sent her a clipping, a quotation from Joyce Carol Oates;

> "One always thinks of a few people, day after day; there's no escape. A father, a mother, a few beloved people—that is the extent of the universe, emotionally. And if something has gone wrong inside this small universe, then nothing can ever be made right."

Long ago, Trudy had given up wanting to be a writer because she could not bear the pressure of words: their intensity. Weaving had seemed like the perfect substitute—a craft, not an art, she could practice and enjoy. But the forces that drive and compose had played their trick on her. From a hundred different skeins ghosts and memories glowed or were subdued in their own mutability. Even the damselfly of that fateful day was there in a range of purples and greens, robbed of its irridescence, but not its richness, by the years between.

For three years she had worked at a job she hated in order to clear her great-grandmother's estate of back taxes and legal fees. But now that the farm was finally her home, she found that the determination which had sustained her through so much had disappeared as quickly as mist from the hillside.

"Am I one of those for whom nothing can ever be made right?" she asked aloud, softly.

There was no one to answer. Around her the fabulous colors of her own making glowed, challenging her like the unknown force in a dream.

ABOUT THE AUTHOR

Bennie Lee Sinclair has received a Stephen Vincent Benet and the Winthrop Award for poetry, and a BEST AMERICAN SHORT STORY citation for fiction. She is an advisory editor of *Appalachian Heritage* magazine.

"The modern world, by multiplying necessities, multiplies the needy, and makes the peaceable practicing of Poverty more and more difficult. ... Whether we wipe out the superfluous poor by cannon-balls, or destroy entire harvests of wheat by fire, or throw tons of mild into the river, they are all identical ways of meeting the situation."

—George Bernanos, A *Diary of My*
Time (New York, 1938), p. 159.

"There is a modern technique of granting assistance to the weak, to the disinherited, to the wretched of all kinds. But from the standpoint of techniques in general, the pure and simple suppression of such people would cost less. Therefore, technology will sooner or later suppress them."

—George Bernanos, *The Last Essays*
of George Bernanos (Chicago, 1955), p. 8.

Appalachia's Path to Welfare Dependency

by
Paul Salstrom

As of 1840 Southern Appalachia figured as one of the most self-sufficient regions of the United States. By 1940 it had become one of the country's *least* self-sufficient regions.

Between 1880 and 1930 the southern mountains experienced a rapid transition toward industrialization. During that half century, the region's self-sufficiency in food production waned.

Late, when industry faltered in the 1930's, the federal govenment provided relief on a massive scale. Relief became so extensive that it brought many mountaineers a degree of economic and social stability that their families had not known for generations—since industrialization began or before—but in the process it also made many mountain farmers more dependent on regular cash income than they had ever previously been. In this paper I will talk only about economic dependency, not about psychological dependency.

Claude Dillion, who was born in 1918 in the Marrowbone Creek neighborhood of Mingo County, West Virginia, and who lived through the Depression there, formed the opinion that "the public works programs that were prescribed to put people to work, simply took them away from farm life, took them away from self-sufficient way to do things."[1] And a storekeeper in the Upper Mud River section of Lincoln County, West Virginia shared that view, saying, "It was the WPA that started farming on its downhill path all around here. The WPA paid farmers to work on roads, and work on this and that, till they started counting on that money and neglecting their land."[2]

New Deal policymakers evidently felt no misgivings about the usefulness of pumping cash into "backward" areas like Appalachia. Harry Hopkins and his colleagues often bucked local political opposition in Appalachia to attain their relief quotas. (The phenomenon of this political opposition in Appalachia cannot be equated with the opposition manifested by the Deep South's oligarchy. Tenancy, share-cropping, and farm wage labor were all pervasive in the Deep South, but were exceptions to the rule in Appalachia. In the Deep South, federal relief became a de facto alternative to low-paid farm labor, but in Appalachia it displaced mainly the traditional localized economic system that I call the "subsistence-barter-and-borrow system." Below, I will go into detail about that system. I believe that it constitutes a crucial part of our "usuable past," and I want to share with you news about rural pockets in which that traditional economic system is being revived, using a model devised two and a half years ago in British Columbia and called the LETS system—the Local Exchange Trading System.

I do not claim that the New Deal *singlehandedly* created Appalachia's dependence on federal transfer payments. That would be an over-simplification. The region's dependency grew gradually, becoming *welfare* dependency only in its last stage.[3] From the beginning, Appalachia's trade with the outside world (consisting of agricultural exports and merchandise imports) depended upon outside capital, and later, industrialization during the 1880–1930 period also depended upon outside investment. In both cases, the main source of investment capital was the Northern United States.[4]

You can say whatever you want about that investment capital. My purpose here is not to moralize but to analyze, and in the late 1920's, when demand for coal quit growing, the coal industry became more competitive, Appalachia was *able* to successfully compete, and its coal capital was not withdrawn. The reason Appalachia could successfully compete, however, was because its miners did not need as much wage (that is, cash) income as their Northern counterparts. The Appalachian miner's lifestyle was more rural than was the Northern miner's. The average Appalachian miner and his family subsisted in part off the land, raising a large garden and keeping some livestock.[5] And because wages could be scaled lower in Appalachia, coal mining here was conducted by more labor-intensive methods.

In 1933, with the New Deal and in particular the National Recovery Administration, wage and price supports were imposed on the country. This penalized labor-intensive operations in favor of those more capital intensive, delivering a blow to not only Appalachian mining but also Piedmont textile manufacturing, and this came at the very time when the Depression had curtailed opportunities to move *out* of the South. The great growth of those Southern industries, remember, had only been possible because they could compete in their respective markets—which they could do only because they did not pay their workers a fully family-supporting wage. Subsistence agriculture (which incidentally is also labor-intensive, since by definition it pays no cash return on cash investment, and thus attracts no capital)—subsistence agriculture had provided the necessary supplement to the low wages and, in Marxist terms, completed the cycle of "reproduction" by reproducing the labor force in the subsistence mode (the household mode of production).

Labor reproduced itself prolifically under these circumstances but soil fertility did not. From the beginning, Scotch-Irish farming customs were not well suited to *so* hilly a topography. The land's diminishing strength yielded diminishing returns, but most mountaineers resisted migration. They stayed put eventually enduring impoverishment and injuring the land.[6] They stayed put, primarily, because they ranked proximity to their parents and siblings higher than individual economic enrichment.

This family-orientation, mind you, was not comparable to a communitarian lifestyle such as exemplified by the Russian *mir* (village commune). Rural Appalachia's basic socioeconomic group was smaller, composed (as one eastern Kentucky case study found) "of two, three, or more family-households that were particularly solitary and bonded together by strong ties of mutual friendship, and frequent visiting exchanges, as well as by ties of kinship. These were primarily groups of siblings' families or of siblings and their parental families." Beyond these family groups (the same study found) there was "little cooperation in common tasks for the good of the whole neighborhood. Few interfamily economic relationships, such as borrowing farm implements or exchanging labor, existed."[7] A similarly pronounced "familism," accompanied by a comparable lack of community cooperation, was discovered by a West Virginia case study.[8]

A decline of community solidarity began quite early, according to the Depression-era union organizer Jim Garland (whose family went back many generations in southeastern Kentucky). Garland writes that "when there remained no more unclaimed farmland to take up, . . . two classes of people emerged. . . . Thus, even before the coal operators came into the region, mountain society had begun to disintegrate."[9]

As their living standard fell in the mountain fastness, many Appalachian farmers gladly went to work for wages that were lower than those paid for the performance of comparable jobs elsewhere in the United States. In the competitive coal industry of the 1920's this proved to be an advantage and Appalachian coal was consistently able to undersell Northern coal until 1933, when the National Recovery Administration's price and wage supports threatened this situation.[10] Appalachia's coal areas then began to grow dependent on federal welfare payments. Capital did not so much take flight from the mountains as it took flight from wages—from labor. It went into making Appalachian mines as capital intensive as Northern mines. Since the coal areas had already become largely cash-dependent before the Depression began, I would have agreed that welfare provision was the best policy for the New Deal to adopt in these coal areas.

By contrast, I believe that in areas where subsistence agriculture was still predominantly practiced full time, federal relief (including work relief under the WPA) produced a great increase in dependency. Through cash injections, such areas were weaned from conditions of relative local autonomy —from local subsistence undergirded by intense family-group networks of borrowing and barter—to a situation in which cash became a pre-condition for a far larger proportion of economic transactions.

In terms of avoiding dependency, what is important about the subsistence-barter-and-borrow system is that (1) it needed to produce no profit on investments which originated outside the region, and (2) it produced its own consumption items and thus (despite a scarcity of cash) wealth was not drained out of the region through heavy purchases. The system's small cash requirement was not onerous. [See Figure.] The system required an initial investment (which was unnecessary for some heirs) to purchase agricultural capital goods—tools, for instance, and also animals and animal-drawn farm implements. After that, the system required just a few dollars annually for tool replacement and a few more for consumption items which were not native to Appalachia. [See Figure.] The only serious obstacle was that the subsistence-borrow-barter system required use of an agriculturally viable piece of land. This could be a daunting obstacle for young people coming up into adulthood but, given adequate land, Appalachian family groups which engaged full time

59

in subsistence farming were virtually autonomous vis--vis economic forces beyond their neighborhoods.

Let me emphasize that Appalachia's full-time subsistence farmers were *not* thus self-sufficient as separate individuals or even as separate conjugal families. Each conjugal family did *not* live by using only the tools or equipment that it personally owned, or by subsisting entirely off the animals and produce that it personally raised. It lived by combining a degree of such self-sufficiency with a prodigious amount of barter and borrowing of both objects and labor. This borrow-and barter activity was continuous (except for occasional feuds) but it did not exist with equal intensity between all residents of a neighborhood. It flourished primarily within family groups as defined above: "two, three, or more family-households" which were generally "groups of siblings' families or of siblings and their parental families." Such family groups drew on resources beyond their own numbers, however, since some of their members were simultaneously members of other family groups (holding multiple membership), and also since some borrowing and barter bore no reference to family groups.

Folklore reveals much about this aspect of rural Appalachian life. Gossip networks are a by-word and there exists an unspoken expectation that everyone will give some account of his goings-on. No one is willingly allowed to shut himself off and to refuse to render a running account of his material life. An economic function lurks barely below the surface of this rural snoopiness, and manifests in the proposals which frequently follow on the heels of prying questions. Having asked "What are you working on these days?" your neighbor may next say, "So in that case you're not using your ladder"—or your winch or your railroad jack. "Reckon then you're not using your railroad jack. Though I might change my sill log." And rather than hire the two or three helpers required to change his sill log, he would expect free help, it being understood that he would return equal labor on request, or repay in goods at a mutually convenient time.

A relatively poor farmer might contribute *mostly* labor within this system, whereas a relatively prosperous farmer might more readily lend equipment. During the Depression, in the least developed neighborhood of Pendleton County, West Virginia, "it was customary for several of the more well-to-do farmers to buy a piece of machinery in common which all their neighbors would use until it wore out, at which time the same persons would purchase another."[11] Probably such equipment lending was balanced to everyone's satisfaction by labor contributions from the poorer families of the neighborhood. All three of Pendleton County's banks had failed in 1931 and the web of barter transactions grew very complex there. Most of the country's merchants and professionals then still raised livestock on the side and were thus able, with little inconvenience, to accept payment in animals and grain.[12]

60

Urbanites have difficulty weighing the contribution made by borrowing and barter to rural life. (And for all their "research," most scholars are urbanites.) Cash is admittedly the most transportable and universal form of asset, but these attributes often hold limited appeal for people who intend to stay where they are, and who share with their fellow locals a very specific environment worked with specific implements. Generalizations about poverty which are based on annual per capita income (even if income "in kind" is included, and home production) reflect urban assumptions about what comprises a standard of living. In the daily affairs of cash-poor farmers, a cash-price citation for something obtainable through barter bears no practical relation to the cash figures on the price tags of items obtainable only through a cash payment.[13] Thus, the workings of a subsistence-barter-and-borrow system cannot be understood through a sequence of equivalents in a different economic system, a system in which cash does often change hands.

If we look beyond farm products (that is, beyond consumption items) and examine the position of productive durables within the two contrasting economic systems, we find the maximum amount of divergence between market-value and use-value. Within a subsistence-barter-and-borrow system, numerous people have access to a tool or implement when they need it, and yet need to possess no equity in the item. Productive durables such as tools and farm implements were borrowed and reborrowed, traded and re-traded, in Appalachia. Cash too circulates at a certain rate, of course, but cash is of no direct use to a person while he holds it. In rural Appalachia, a tool or a plow has exchange value, like cash, but in addition it has direct productive value. Subsistence production, borrowing, and barter (including labor barter) operated in Appalachia as a unified system. No one of these activities would have been of so much benefit without the other two.[14]

What significance does all this have? Is it purely academic?

How we measure things influences how we value them. It is impossible, even today, to measure the *real income* of the Appalachian region or of any part of it, for we have no quantifying yardstick to render a subsistence-barter-borrow system even roughly comparable to the cash system. Without a quantified comparison, urbanites (including most scholars) will continue to puzzle over the supposedly "self-limiting" (or, to their partisans, "selfless") features of Appalachian thought and behavior. We will continue to confuse ways of life with standards of living, as does no less a thinker than Rupert Vance in his introduction to *The Southern Appalachian Region: A Survey*. Vance says that the New Deal's "standards made at least half the population in certain Appalachian areas eligible for relief" which in turn "introduced the people to the money economy and increased their wants. The depression, then, actually served to raise standards for many families in the region who had lacked contact with the

61

American standard of living." Vance does hasten to add that the Depression "left the region with a high rate of relief and a low basis for economic security," but he lets stand his implicit equation of "the American standard of living" with a *raised* standard and not merely with "the money system."[15]

You can go further left in the political spectrum and still find such clichs where there should be analysis. The clich "self-sufficing farm" is no more examined among the romantic left which lauds the image (Scott and Helen Nearing, et al.) than among the revolutionary left which disparages it. But unitl the left begins to economically disassociate itself from the American economic behemoth, its protest against that behemoth will remain largely symbolic. True, we cannot be self-sufficing as single individuals or as separate conjugal families. At the other extreme, however, if we organize economically on too grand a scale we will inevitably be co-opted. Michael Linton, the British Columbian who organized the first LETS barter system, suggests that fifty to two hundred people is the ideal size for a non-cash system of economic exchange. LETS stands for "Local Exchange Trading System" and the system functions as a combination information network and cashless bank. Each member of a LETS system has an account and receives monthly statements of what their "balance" is—that is, whether their account is in debit or credit, and how much. In the system as a whole, debits must equal credits, since every exchange (whether of labor or of goods) is debited to the receiving person and credited to the providing person. The value of each exchange is determined by mutual agreement between its receiver and its provider. The first LETS system employs a computer to facilitate bookkeeping. A telephone answering machine is used to record the members' transactions, and once a day the transactions are entered into the computer.

As for the "information network" aspect of the system, this consists of a monthly sheet which reports the goods and services currently offered by each member, with prices cited in dollars. This sheet is mailed out each month to each member along with his "statement." (Like a bank statement, the LETS statement is a computer print-out which reports all the transactions of the past month, and the balance of the account.) A supplemental information sheet can be issued to tell members of each other's needs, like a want-ad sheet.[16] The applicability of this updated version of old-fashioned barter is obvious in the cash-poor sections of Appalachia. How often the lack of money prevents a rational and humane distribution of goods and services! What LETS does is to extend the traditional circle of barter, so that people can exchange goods and services *indirectly*. You may not *directly* need what someone else has to barter. Through a LETS system, you can barter with them *indirectly*, using the entire system's membership as intermediaries. In my own country, I know, this will prove a great boon, expecially to the new homesteaders how have settled there.

ENDNOTES

1. Quoted in Michael T. Tierney, "Bread on the Water: Education in an Isolated Mountain Community," *Human Services in the Rural Environment* 8, no. 3 (Winter 1983):7.

2. June 1983 interview by the writer with Ray Gene Black, manager of Black Brothers General Merchandise at Myra, West Virginia.

3. For a concise summation of dependency theory, see Richard White, *The Roots of Dependency: Subsistence, Environment, and Social Change Among the Choctaws, Pawnees, and Navajos* (Lincoln: University of Nebraska Press, 1983), pp. xv-xix. As a definition, White quotes Theotonio Dos Santos:

   By dependency we mean a situation in which the economy of certain countries is conditioned by the development and expansion of another economy to which the former is subjected. The relation of interdependence between two or more economies, and between these and world trade, assumes the form of dependence when some countries (the dominant ones) can expand and be self-sustaining, while other countries (the dependent ones) can do this only as a reflection of that expansion, which can have either a positive or negative effect on their immediate development. (Quoted in Richard White, p. xvii.)

4. As regards the dependence of Appalachia's early commerce on Northern capital, see Lewis E. Atherton, *The Southern Country Store, 1800–1860* (Baton Rouge: Louisiana State University Press, 1949) pp. 129–34. On Northern capital sources for Appalachia's industrialization, see Ronald D. Eller, *Miners, Millhands, and Mountaineers: Industrialization of the Appalachian South, 1880–1930* (Knoxville: University of Tennessee Press, 1982), pp. 134–53.

5. David Alan Corbin, *Life, Work, and Rebellion in the Coal Fields: The Southern West Virginia Miners, 1880–1922* (Urbana: University of Illinois Press, 1981), pp. 33–35.

6. With more rational farming methods, Appalachia's fertility need not have been squandered. A 1916 article, "Farming Appalachia" by J. Russell Smith, challenged America's vast agricultural research establishment of that day to "develop and teach a mountain agriculture that will make the mountaineer prosperous and leave him his mountain." After a world tour to study hill-farming methods, Smith recommended "good little permanent terraced fields" such as he had found in Corsica. He also encouraged tree planting to provide fruits, nuts, and seeds, putting emphasis on "the mulberry, the persimmon, the honey locust, the acorn, and the chestnut, [which] are primarily forage crops, chiefly pig feed, but also good for poultry, sheep, goats, and cows." As forest-grown human foods, Smith recommended walnuts and pecans. Smith emphasized that hog-forage crops should received priority in Appalachia, since Appalachia's people were used to eating pork, and any surplus of hogs could be marketed. See J. Russell Smith, "Farming Appalachia," *American Review of Reviews* 53, no. 3 (March 1916):329–36. Smith's suggestions (which also included pawpaw trees) remain excellently suited to Appalachia. For general ideas on sustainable agriculture for hill regions, see J.R. Smith, *Tree Crops* (Old Greenwich, Conn.: Devin-Adair, 1950); and J. Sholto Douglas and Robert A. de J. Hart, *Forest Farming* (London: Watkins, 1976).

7. Harry K. Schwarzweller, James S. Brown, and J.J. Mangalam, *Mountain Families in Transition: A Case Study of Appalachian Migration* (University Park: Pennsylvania State University Press, 1971), p. 40.

8. John Craft Taylor, "Depression and the New Deal in Pendleton: A History of a West Virginia County from the Great Crash to Pearl Harbor, 1929-1941," Ph.D. dissertation, Pennsylvania State University, 1980, pp. 124-27, 133.

9. *Welcome the Traveler Home: Jim Garland's Story of the Kentucky Mountains*, ed. Julia S. Audrey (Lexington: University Press of Kentucky, 1983), pp. 18-19.

10. It might be some consolation if one could think that, while marginalizing Appalachia's coal, the National Recovery Administration anyway did help the United States ecomony as a whole. But it has now been shown that the price supports written into the NRA's codes completely negated an 8 percent annual GNP growth which otherwise would have flowed from the 14 percent monetary expansion created by Roosevelt's gold policy. See Michael Weinstein, *Recovery and Redistribution under the NIRA* (Amsterdam: North-Holland, 1980), pp. 273-79.

11. Information from 1973 interviews used in John Craft Taylor, "Depression and New Deal in Pendleton," p. 130.

12. Taylor, "Depression and the New Deal in Pendleton," p. 819.

13. In a classic article, Michael Merrill made this point by saying that money-of-account does not function the same as money. See Michael Merrill, "Cash Is Good To Eat: Self-Sufficiency and Exchange in the Rural Economy of the United States," *Radical History Review* 5(Winter 1977):56. But it is important not to forget that there are *points of reference* between the cash system and the subsistence-borrow-barter system. As Karl Polanyi reminds us, "unless [a market] pattern is present, at least in patches, the propensity to barter will find insufficient scope: it cannot produce prices.... The principle of barter depends for its effectiveness on the market pattern." Karl Polany, *The Great Transformation* (Boston: Beacon Press, 1957), p. 56.

14. Among the *urban* poor, barter and borrowing has also routinely occurred—in their case without subsistence production. An exemplary analysis is Ellen Ross, "Survival Networks: Women's Neighborhood Sharing in London Before World War One," *History Workshop* 15(1983):4-27.

15. Rupert B. Vance, "The Region: A New Survey," in *The Southern Appalachian Region: A Survey*, ed. Thomas R. Ford (Lexington: University of Kentucky Press, 1962), p.5.

16. Susan Meeker-Lowry, "The Local Exchange Trading Systems," *Green Revolution* 42, no. 3 (Fall 1985):1-2.

Past Commitments, Current Problems, and Future Choices: Water Resources in Appalachia

by
Dennis L. Soden

Preface

This paper is the first step in studying water-related issues in the Appalachian region. As a transplanted westerner who has focused almost entirely on water policy issues in the western states, the author attempts in this paper to summarize initial reaction to the state of water resource issues and management mechanisms in Appalachia. Further, a glimpse at what may lay in waiting for the Appalachian region if water resource use and development are not placed high on the political agenda is developed. As a goal, a better feel for potential conflict which may come to the fore and a choice of options which may be available to natural resource administrators and civic leaders is sought.

Introduction

A struggle is developing in the Appalachian Region about how to best manage the region's vital water resources. At the core of this developing struggle are increased water use patterns incompatible with past and existing standards.

Southern mountain people have a reputation for their jealous efforts to preserve their environment's quality and natural resources (Schoenbaum, 1979). As population increases, new demands are placed on water

65

resources. Without too much speculation, we can safely say that these emerging demands will create widespread water supply problems in the eastern United States.[1] As this problem develops, public attention will increasingly focus upon water use and water development policies. Thus, it is both appropriate and timely to make an assessment of water policy practices and opportunities as a first step in searching for a future which nurtures development while maintaining the region's resources.

This paper will attempt to put the present period—a period of "transition"—into perspective. This transition in water policy and management has been characterized as a period in which an "appropriate balance between water quantity and quality aspects" has not been achieved (Hufschmidt, 1979:1). This paper does not attempt to be definitive. The field of water policy is complex, interdisciplinary and dominated by technical, scientific and legal considerations. A grasp of the system can, however, be obtained. The basic policy issues are not any more difficult to analyze than those of pollution control, toxic and nuclear waste disposal or land-use policy, all topics of current concern in the region.

Four areas of water policy important to the discussion of Appalachia are considered in this paper. First, existing water law which serves as the major management mechanism is reviewed. Second, the potential for conflict which exists as part of water use and development will be addressed, particularly the instream verses consumptive nature of water usage. Third, a consideration of major management concepts which exist in the current natural resource and environmental policy literature will be undertaken. These natural resource management concepts will be evaluated for their practicality in a riparian doctrine situation like that existing in the Southern Appalachians. Fourth, a management concept for "safe development" of the region's natural resources—a community-based model, based on the work of leading water policy scholars Stephen B. Mumme and Helen Ingram will be forwarded. Fifth and last, implications for future research into this salient issue will be forwarded.

Water Law: The Stage for Water Resources Use and Development

The states of the Southern Appalachians embrace a mixture of water rights systems. In nearly every state, the common law water rights of the past have proved inadequate in water scarce environments (Ausness, 1983:547). Consequently, the common law rules relied upon in the past have "typically" been either supplemented or replaced by some form of statutory water allocation system. The success or failure of the present system has been discussed elsewhere (Ausness, 1983) and this paper does not attend to a full description of water law practices (see instead; Trelease, 1979; Cox, 1982). As an aid in understanding the issue, however, a brief review of water law is given here.

66

Historically, in the area of surface water which this paper focuses upon in general, the riparian system of water law has prevailed in the eastern United States. In contrast, the western states have adopted the prior appropriation system in its different forms.[2] The riparian system of water law was developed from English common law and subsequently reflects the cummulative decisions of the courts of that heritage. Simply, under a riparian system, rights to use of water are obtained from ownership of land bordering natural water courses. The use of riparian water is restricted to the land bordering the water course—the riparian land. Two concepts direct the riparian water order. First, riparian landowners are entitled, via the "natural flow doctrine," to have water flow through their land in its natural condition—not restricted or polluted except from normal domestic uses or upstream riparians. Non-domestic use is permitted, only if a perceivable dimunition in natural flow is absent (Cox, 1982:110–111).

The second concept is the "reasonable use rule." The rule allows each riparian to make any use of the water provided that his use is reasonable relative to the needs of other riparians. Reasonableness is a gray area of the law and provides a context for both conflict and conflict resolution whenever one riparian user feels injured by another.

Until the accelerated population growth and economic development of the last four decades, which has been even more pronounced in the last decade in the Appalachians, riparian doctrine sufficed since there was a plentiful natural supply of both surface and groundwater (Howells and Grigg, 1978:2).

Dissatisfaction with the common law and riparian system has led a number of Appalachian states to consider adoption of statutory system of water rights. The states of North Carolina, South Carolina, Georgia, and West Virginia have given serious consideration to abandoning the riparian system in favor of appropriation standards used in the western United States. While only Mississippi among eastern states has actually adopted the appropriation doctrine, virtually all eastern states, including those of the Appalachian region have incorporated a portion of the prior appropriation system into their new permit systems (Ausness, 1983: 554).

In basic terms, a fundamental shift has been made which enables non-riparian landowners, previously unable to hold water rights, to perfect a water right by obtaining a water use permit. In the Appalachians, this is the case in Virginia and is considered to be implied in Kentucky (Ausness, 1983:554). The permit system which emerged in the 1970s and which continues to develop in various forms in the states of Georgia, Kentucky, North Carolina, South Carolina, and Virginia, provides for a state agency to administer water rights programs. Perfecting a water right requires successfully obtaining a permit from the state. The permit may be denied if other water users are adversely affected or if the "public interest" is threatened. A permit system is the first step in the adoption of the prior appropriation system, but unlike the west, in the east water rights are not held in perpetuity. In addition, water rights are not transferable to other landowners in the eastern modification. Instead they are appurtenants to the land (Ausness, 1983:553) which are attached to the property declared in the permit.

Political Conflicts Among Water Users

In the brief discussion of water law and changes which may impact the Appalachian region, the uses of water have not been considered. What characterizes an allocation system like that used in western states is the development of statutory priority to water use as a means of resolving conflict. In the east this event has yet to occur, largely due to legislative refusals to explicitly address the difficult and complex issues inherent when states allocate resources. For regional observers of the Appalachians, this means that regionally held water may in the future be declared surplus—water not being put to its most beneficial use. Consequently, the large quantity of Appalachian water which we can safely say most presently is taken for granted, may become the object of downstream interests, short in both quality and quantity of water.

Despite the evolution which is occurring in eastern water law, designed to deal with emerging problems occassioned by water development, there exists considerable potential for conflict among competing water users. Figure 1 displays some water resource uses which have been recognized as "beneficial uses." Figure 1 over simplifies, but demonstrates potential conflict which residents and natural resource managers in the region must be aware of.

The cells in Figure 1 indicate the impact of a particular use upon other uses. It is important to note those uses which are incompatible with each other; these are the areas where the greatest conflict may be expected to emerge.

This is a subjective chart, and the reader may disagree with some cells or envision impacts which are not noted. The intent is not to imply that proper management cannot accomodate multiple uses, but to underscore likely conflicts.

Beneficial uses have been grouped into consumptive and non-consumptive categories. Consumptive water uses are those which take water from a waterway and do not directly return it (municipal, industrial and irrigation uses for example). Return flows may seep into groundwater, into different stream, or return to the same stream in reduced quality and very often in reduced quantity. In contrast, non-consumptive uses include those which divert water from a stream and immediately return it (fish hatcheries, hydroelectric power and those uses in the stream such as instream recreation).

Consumptive uses tend to conflict with one another and with non-consumptive uses. The severity of this impact depends primarily on the volume of water withdrawn. If non-consumptive uses were maximized, they would obviously be in conflict with consumptive ones. Further, many non-consumptive uses may be incompatible with each other (industry/wastewater with preservation/recreation).

The perspective given in Figure 1 can be viewed in light of the discussion of water law. The development of a permit system may establish priorities based on date, not type of use. The permit system as "textbook" designed is neutral among water uses except in times of scarcity. Consequently, a neutral system may hold considerable potential for harm to certain uses by other, unknowingly and indirectly, as well as directly.

Figure 1. Potential Conflicts Among Water Users

	Domestic	Agri-culture (irrigation)	Energy	Transport-ation	Indus-trial	Recre-ation	Preservation (Esthetics)
Domestic		-	-			-	-
Agriculture (irrigation)	-		-	-	-	-	-
Energy	-	-			+	-	-
Transportation		-			+		
Industrial		-	+	+		-	-
Recreation	-	-	-		-		+
Preservation (Esthetics)	-	-	-		-	+	

+ = Compatible or Beneficial
- = Incompatible or Harmful

Contemporary Appalachia is experiencing a transition in population and demography, in addition ot changes in the use of natural resources like water. Simultaneously, parallel changes are occurring in our institutional mechanisms for managing resources. For the Appalachians, the critical question must be asked, *can changes in water law be perfected in*

69

time to service and resolve conflict likely to arise among new and competing users in a transition era? The answer to this question is not easily attained. A system of management for the region's water resources requires a coordinating, comprehensive, planning policy process as the most efficient means of implementing decisions regarding both development and preservation of resources. The move toward permit systems has been heralded as a significant and important first step (Ausness, 1983:589). Nevertheless, many deficiencies exist. A water use and development scheme requires a "gameplan," "framework" or, in the jargon of the academic, a "theoretical thrust" to direct policymaking.1 The next section will discuss the most dominiant conceptual frameworks which are used in natural resource policy today. By looking at these frameworks a sense of alternative water resource use and development futures is obtained. Without consideration of these policymaking and planning alternatives, a "primitive and incomplete" view of the issue is obtained and conflict is more probable.

Approaches to Water Resource Management: Contending Views

A central issue concerning water use and development in the Appalachian region, as in any other, is the need to develop consistent analytical devices. Put another way, it is paramount that a "gameplan" be formulated for water resources use and developmen. In this section two of the more commonly used resource management frameworks are reviewed. Following this, a third framework is put forward in light of the unique social, economic and political characteristics which the Appalachian region holds. This exercise may seem frivolous or trivial to many, however, only by beginning to promote discussion of what could become one of the most serious problems we face regionally and nationally in the next decade—water resources management—steps in the right direction may be taken (Congressional Quarterly, 1981). The two models reviewed include: first, the model of the "Commons," and second, the private ownership approach labeled "new resource economics" by scholars in the field. In response to these a derivative of the public choice approach called community-based management will be proposed as an alternative for water resource management for Appalachia's future.

THE COMMONS MODEL. One consideration of water development and protection brings to light the classic questions of equitable choice—namely who plays and who doesn't pay for development or protection, pollution and degradation versus preservation and aesthetics. In the case discussed here, the "common property resource" belonging to the Appalachian community is the set of water resources, whose devel-

70

opment or protection can politically benefit or cost all or none in one way or another. The attainment of community-wide benefits requires that disproportionate costs be borne by some citizens, while at the same time greater benefits accrue to some than to others. The decision to undertake management of water resources is based on a belief in the common property aspects—that each citizen has a right to access of some portion of a potentially diminishing resource. The decision to avoid what we have come to know, in natural resource and other policy fields, as a "Tragedy of Commons" (Hardin, 1968) is a situation where "the remorseless working of things leads individuals, acting in their own best interest, to produce joint consequences not in their long-term interest (Hardin, 1968)[3].

Appalachian water resources are an excellent example of a commons, in as much as: (1) ownership of the resource is subject to many common ownership characteristics (i.e., the flow of streams past numerous riparian land holders, or the sharing of groundwater pools); (2) a large number of users are exercising independent rights to the resource (i.e., through riparian rights or permit systems); (3) no other user is able to effectively control the activites of others without utilization of specified instructional mechanisms (i.e., the court system), and; (4) in the long-term, total demand upon the resource will exceed the capacity of the common resourceto provide benefits (Hardin, 1968).

In a commons dilemma, recognition of a pending crisis within the area eventually triggers community decsions to formulate plans and to initiate development of commons management institutions as a way of responsibly managing the available resources for the "benefit of the community." Presently, the characteristic "commons" nature of Appalachian water resources has been only partially recognized. Few efforts to achieve collective action among regional neighbors to avert Hardin's predicted "tragedy" exist, but as they say there is no better time than the present to begin.[4]

If institutional measures designed to protect the region's water resources from overuse are not implemented, the commons will be exhausted and each individual will lose the economic or intangible values associated with use of the resource (Ciriacy-Wantrup, 1975). In the case of Appalachian water resources, government intervention at the state, interstate-regional, as well as local levels is required to prevent overuse and excess degradation of the resource. The Commons Model is popular and intuitively makes sense. It has a long and rich history among natural resource managers and scholars. Recently, however, it has been challenged by a new wave of literature which also focuses upon institutional needs required for the management of scarce national resources.

NEW RESOURCE ECONOMICS. The New Resource Economics school of thought has been characterized by one commentator as "an almost libertarian outpouring of market-oriented recommendations for allocating water" (Griffin, 1984). From the New Resource Economics perspective water shortage comes about because of the lack of a balance between supply and demand, not a shortage of total available water. Water is treated as any other ecomonic commodity and proponents of the school propose that water shortages, in either quality or quantity, can be solved by transferring the commondity from lower to higher valued uses (Andersen, 1983; Mumme and Ingram, 1984). Proponents of this view suggest that the existing institutions (i.e., government management, especially at the state level) act as an impediment to "accurate translation of society's real preference for water use" (Mumme and Ingram, 1984:1).

A recent and influential book by Terry L. Anderson exemplifies this perspective:

> Water prices have been kept below market clearing levels, and the inevitable shortages have followed. The government has responded by attempting to constrain demand, ration water, and increase the available supply. Except in isolated cases where shortages have been caused by drought and where a cooperative community spirit has developed, efforts to ration water have not been successful. Increased water supplies have only been possible though the construction of massive water projects, which have dammed many of our free-flowing rivers and built thousands of miles of aqueducts. These projects have been extremely costly, and it is questionable whether funds for them will continue to be available. Without a price mechanism operating on water supply and demand, crisis situations will continue to arise (Andersen, 1983:5).

Andersen, one of the "gurus" of this movement, prescribes developing a free market for water, whereby individual property rights over water would supersede state or other government's control. The "crisis" of water shortage could be dealt with by prices sufficiently attractive to bid water away from owners whose uses are of low value.

This literature adopts very strong value positions at odds with traditional thinking about water. Obviously, considering water as a commodity which can be privately traded is in sharp contrast to the long-standing notions that water is a commons good or public good, with special characteristics meeting needs which are not "practically" dealt with in market transactions (Soden, 1986). Further, the New Resource Economics recommendation seriously threatens the interest of some poor, rural groups who view the control over water as essential to community security, self-determination, and culture and lifestyle. Much of the Appalachian region, it can be contended, is represented by communities with these attributes.

This study critically examines the basic assumptions of New Resource Economics with respect to Appalachian water resources and suggests that the commons model has greater validity. The commons model in conjuction with an alternative framework—community-based management—may provide a means more amendable to the communities of the Appalachian region.

It is also useful to note that New Resource Economics has gained political appeal at the same time as the beneficiaries of federal intervention (money supply to large scale water development projects) have shifted. As Stephen Mumme and Helen Ingram suggest:

> It is widely conceded that the era of water development has given way to one of water management where available water is *reallocated* among users rather than new supplies being developed. Few new projects are being authorized which serve the interest of developmental constituencies (Mumme and Ingram, 1984:4, emphasis added).

We are entering a period where other interests who have not previously shared in the benefits of federal water projects are beginning to assert themselves. More specifically, as water demands have pressed close upon available supplies, *Appalachia may hold the water necessary to alleviate crisis elsewhere.* Interbasin transfers of water are now practical and have reached the South, as evidenced by the effort of the Virginia Beach/Newport News and other Virginia areas to obtain needed water supplies from Lake Gaston on the Virginia-North Carolina border (Cox and Shubman 1985; Walker and Bridgeman, 1985). Is Appalachian water next? New Resource Economics proposes that we transfer institutional control to individuals and "radically decentralize water policymaking" a move which could have dramatic and perhaps damaging implications for the Appalachian region.[5]

The present, which many suggest is a time of transition in the Appalachians, may provide a useful case for evaluating New Resource Economics and to suggest an alternative management framework for development and use of the region's water resources.

73

Searching for Alternatives: Community-Based Management

The incompatablity between the New Resource Economics approach and water resource allocation problems in the Appalachian region can be demonstrated. The political plight of the many low-income rural communities of the Appalachians, and the importance of control over water resources, can be illustrated by drawing parallels from John Gaventa's work, *Power and The Powerlessness* (1980). Gaventa discusses the lack of political power among the historically less-advantaged communities, and the continued economic poverty which prevails in much of the region. Gaventa sees three aspects of political power in the Appalachians: (1) their participation in politics is ineffective for reasons relating to a lack of economic resources, lack of political skills, poor political strategy and failure to build support; (2) they are excluded from channels of participation by existing biases in the political system, values of elite decision-makers or procedural biases within the political system; and, (3) they are exluded because these communities themselves accept the policy norms of the prevailing system as their own, contrary to their material and cultural interest, and thus acquiesce in their exclusion from the political and policy process systems. Gaventa's explanations have been used to study the politics of water use in the western United States, particualrly the water crisis which has come to the fore on the numerous Indian reservations in the Southwest (Ingram and Mumme, 1984, 1985). It is appropriate that it come home to roost, so to speak, and be a source for discussion of water politics attendant to the Appalachians.

Gaventa's first explanation emphasizes the importance of economic and political resources as a base of political power and influence. Water has long standing political and economic value, especially when conditions of prior appropriation and permits exist. Further, water is closely linked to political cohesion (Soden, 1985a; Mumme and Ingram, 1984, 1985; Pierce and Lovrich, 1980).

Water is not a commodity which is absent of special meaning for a community, but is indeed a "different kind of resource with effects and significance beyond its material value. Water has been described as a "fundamental social resource" (Mumme and Ingram, 1984:26). Its social characteristic links it inextricably to economic and political power, social welfare and equity, community security, cultural cohesion, and the nature of economic and social change wihtin a community (Mumme and Ingram, 1984:26). Along this line of reasoning, Robert and Eva Hunt conclude that " . . . there is a strong case to be made for a linkage between control over water resources and control over other decisions in the local unit (Hunt and Hunt, 1976).

Other findings by researchers in the water politics field point to the connection between control over water resources and levels of public

74

participation (Maas and Andersen; Ingram, et. al., 1980; Pierce and Doerkson, 1976). Rural communities's control over water use and development has been recognized as a strong incentive which obtains political cohesion. The most powerful conclusion which has emerged from a number of case studies of rural water issues is the extent to which water users in these communities seek control over their destinies and the use of their resources (Mumme and Ingram, 1984:27; Soden, 1985a).

Control over water resources is a primary source of political power, organization and political participation for low income rural communities. Maintaining and reinforcing this control is likely to be crucial for the survival, or development of some communities and is an important base upon which communities can build political influence and pursue economic development vital to their community's interest whether those interests be monetary or non-monetary in value (Soden, 1986).

Gaventa's second explanation for the lack of politcal power of poor rural communities relates to the bias of political institutions particularly as it affects what issues are placed upon the political agenda for solution. The literature on water law and perfection of water rights illustrates a dynamic process; a process which will greatly affect the Appalachian region. There does not exist, nor is there a major effort to impose a single regulatory system over the nation's or the region's water resources, although efforts to move in this direction exist. The federal rule in the area of water policy has been historically limited to ensuring water rights exist to support federal water projects. However, a growth in the interest in and number of interstate compacts and the federal government's role in negotiation of water disputes, looms on the future. Further, as eastern states turn more and more towards a permit system with similarities to the western states appropriation doctrine, federal claims under the Winter's Doctrine (which allows for federal rights over water resources), may be part of the long term public agenda. States' institutions, laws and regulations predominate, but their focus, more often that not, is on ways to enhance the large population centers "down-the-mountain." As in other parts of the nation, state boundaries and institutions do not serve the broader needs of the region. The area which includes northern Idaho's panhandle, western Montana and eastern Washington is an example of a region (known as the Inland Empire in the Northwest) which maintains unique regional concerns unattended to by political instiutions of both the state and federal governments designed to service the area. Further, it might safely be suggested that an Appalachian regionalism exists and, that as a region, the Appalachians are often overlooked or not recognized by the political instiutions which govern them. As a result, water policy and planning at both the state and federal levels may involve decisions which may adversely affect the region. As demands are pressing closer to supplies, uncertainty threatens to deprive regional control over water resource.

This issue is far from the top of the political agenda. Given the nature of the multiple agenda which exists in environmental politics about water usage (Soden, 1985b) the result may be that when the issues of water use and development do rise to the top of the agenda they will not be framed in a way which proves beneficial to the region. This appropriately introduces Gaventa's third face of power.

Gaventa explains that powerless people tend to be highly dependent and susceptible to the "internalization of values of the dominant." Put another way, they accept the definitions of political reality as offered by the dominant classes or governmental institutions (Gaventa, 1980:17). Until recently, the issue of water in the Appalachians has been framed in terms of water quality or "pork barrel," whereby federal government monies were made available to localities which had political support and a worthy project. In general, water quality was a non-issue, mainly on the grounds that the time was not ripe for politicalization of water.

Currently, the political reality is changing. Water transfers are suggested as replacements for federal development projects, as sources of water to alleviate problems in water shy or poor water quality stricken areas. With this in mind, New Resource Economics would suggest use of an economic efficiency criterion as the governing process. Viewed from Gaventa's perspective, a set of normative tenets, such as those of New Resource Economics, to the extent to which they prevail or act as guideposts in the larger political system, may "well underwrite the exclusion of low income rural communities from participation in the policy process," perpetuating political and economic relations among a core (urban-metropolitan) and its periphery (rural poor).

Since Graham Allison's (1971) seminal study of the Cuban Missile Crisis, political scientists have recognized that the choice of framework for evaluation of political alternatives is far from benign. Instead, the choice of analytic framework influences the interests that are considered legitimate, the information that is relevant, and the values and conclusions drawn. The application of New Resource Economics, based on notions of economic man to water resources, biases the definition of public interest in water rights and disregards the non-mobilized rural poor. Ingram and Mumme have proposed in their studies of Indian communities in the southwestern United States, that a different, more community-oriented mode of analysis would be more appropriate. Table I illustrates the characteristics of the community-oriented mode as compared with the "pop" New Resource Economics.

Community-oriented analysis relies heavily upon political and bureaucratic approaches to policymaking. While rational action based models have proved useful, as Allison notes (1971:5), "there is powerful evidence that it must be supplemented, if not supplanted, by frames of reference that focus on the governmental machine—the organization and political actors involved in the policy process."

TABLE 1.

Alternative Frameworks for Analyzing Water Policies and Institutions

	New Resource Economics	Community-Oriented Analysis
Basis of the Interest	Individual	Group or Collective
Nature of the Interest	Material and Quantifiable	Affective and Symbolic
Basis of Decision Making	Instrumental to Maximizing Individual Benefit	Support and Maintenance of Institutions; Conformity to Norms and Practices
Mode of Interaction	Strategic Action to Maximize Private Interest	Reciprocity, Sharing and Cooperation
Participation	A Cost Incurred In Obtaining Relevant Information To Make Individual Exchanges	An Intrinsic Good That Increases Sense of Belonging; Community Self-Determination
Arenas for Action	Markets and Individualized Exchanges	Politics and Administrative Processes

Source: Mumme and Ingram, 1984

Ingram and Mumme's community-based approach recognizes the group, rather than the individual as the basic unit of interest (Mumme and Ingram, 1984:29). This fits the issue of water resource management which historically, even in the most riparian situations, has been regarded as a community or "common" resource. Within rural communities, Maas and Andersen observe that there have evolved strong traditions of community control over water resources stemming from the desire to maintain the integrity of the social and economic community. In these communities protection from injury results when the actions of individuals promote values which pertain specifically to their communities. The result is the loss of valuable water resources from the community as a whole. This point has clearly emerged at some points in time having been expressed cyclically in Appalachian natural resource politics, including water (Soden with Wilson, 1986). Consequently, it can be expected to return as the "stakes" become higher.

The collective mode of analysis is far more emotional and symbolic rather than purely objective and material. In this regard, water is valued by communities not primarily for the economic return, but for what it means for security and community self-determination.

The community-oriented perspective on water management relies on the notion that rationality is a social and political process of collective evolution, consent, and action. From one community to another this process may vary considerably, ranging from "informal councils to the establishment of tasks force and water districts" (Mumme and Ingram, 1984:30). Whatever the form, this collective action essentially serves, to varying degrees, the individual interests of the members of the community. Community values are reinforced in teh process, galvanizing the citizenry as well as providing the potential for innovation and adaptation by the community body.

The basis for decision-making in the community-oriented analysis model emphasizes reciprocity, sharing, and cooperation in contrast to market procedures, which reward egoistic pursuit of one's own interests. In the community-oriented model altruistic values tend to provide the glue for community bonds. Systems of mutual cooperation "encourage individual participation and responsibility, mutual trust, and nurture a sense of security and equity with the community" (Ingram and Mumme, 1984:31). The result is diminished conflict and increased social cohesion within the community itself.

Participation is not seen simply as a cost to the individual, but as an opportunity for individual development and strengthing of community bonds. "Empowerment" is the term Gaventa proposes for the solidarity fostered by reciprocal, cooperative relations. As a collective body, communities have the strength to hang onto their water resources and to distribute them in ways more serving their social, as well as, economic goals (Maas and Andersen, 1978:368). Repeatedly, studies have shown that rural communities, when they perceive threats to their water resources by actions of outside actors behave in this way (Soden, 1985a; Maas and Andersen, 1978; Mumme and Ingram, 1984, 1985).

Contrary to New Resource Economics, distrust of government, and politics in water management, a community-based approach views politics and administrative processes as essential. As Ingram and Mumme note, low income rural communities outside the political mainstream face political and economic challenge by those seeking to secure abstract entitlements to their resources or otherwise enlarge their resource base. These communities, by definition lack the economic clout to obtain equal treatment through the marketplace (Mumme and Ingram, 1984: 32). The communities of "Appalachia" are often removed from mainstream politics and are economically non-competitive. Subsequently, they must learn to use their community solidarity as a resource to participate in the political and administrative system, to lobby, and to negotiate and influence political activism and collective action is no panacea, indeed it entails risk, but it does afford the possibility of building on the basic political resources of hertofore non-mobilized rural communities to achieve greater equity.

Conclusions

In reviewing the conflict among water resource use and development which may arise in the Southern Appalachians and the changes in eastern water law, it is apparent that water issues could become politically salient. Obviously, lawmakers and policymakers view water issues as part of the political agenda in the South as the permit system continues to develop.

Historically, water resources have been viewed as a commons in many areas, but more recently have been challenged by free market economists through the literature of New Resource Economics. The New Resource Economics movement proposes to alleviate water problems by radically decentralizing control over water resource decision-making and by employing market mechanisms. If these proposals gain wide support, the interests of rural communities—politically and economically poor— could be adversely affected. This paper has examined the policy model of the commons and proposes that a community-oriented process under assumptions of collective action will best serve the long term interests of Appalachians better than will New Resource Economics.

Water is a "fundamental social resource." Globally, social values such as security, equity, and community self-determination have been more important than economic efficiency, particularly in the management of water. Successfully laying claim to and managing water is a challenge and an opportunity for the Appalachians, especially as the current legal system attendant to water rights undergoes fundamental change. For the people of the Appalachians, participation in the legal and political process necessary to secure water resources can be a process of empowerment in the present political environment, empowerment unattainable under the scheme of New Resource Economics.

The proposal or prescription of a community-oriented framework, by which collective action to protect the region's resources emerges, can be a first step in the process of securing a viable future for the region, as it relates to water resources. The community-based proposal draws on the insights of experienced Appalachian scholars like John Gaventa to better understand the political, administrative and economic processes which may parallel experiences in the water resource issues area when the regional residents are short on political and economic clout, and hopefully lay a framework for establishment of policy direction at the subnational level as we search for a future in the Appalachians.

79

ENDNOTES

1. As Richard Ausness (1983) points out, according to estimates, by the end of this century, only three of the 18 federally designated water regions in the continental United States will be able to live comfortably with their water supplies. See also, "Is U.S. Running Out Of Water?," U.S. News and World Report, July 18, 1977:33.

2. The two basic forms of appropriation doctrine include: the "Colorado Doctrine" under which riparian rights are not recognized in the western states of Alaska, Arizona, Colorado, Idaho, Montana, Nevada, New Mexico, Utah, and Wyoming. Under the "California Doctrine," riparian rights may co-exist with appropriative water rights. State following this doctrine include California, Kansas, Nebraska, North Dakota, Oklahoma, Oregan, South Dakota, Texas and Washington (See Ausness, 1983:548). Because riparian and appropriative systems are not particularly compatible, most "California Doctrine" states place limitations on the exercise of riparian rights (Trelease, 1954).

3. The Garret Hardin example (1968) is best known of the conventional views on thinking about common property. Hardin tells a parable about a pasture that is open for use by all with no restrictions. Each person grazing livestock on the pasture looks only at the private benefits and costs of grazing. All the additional benefits of adding an addititional animal to the pasture are captured by the owner of the animal, while the costs of reduced forage are spread to all users. The results are overgrazing and the depletion of the commons.

   The original development of the economics of free and open access is Gordon's (1954) discussion of fisheries as common property resources.

4. The most visible exception to regional action is the forces which collectively acted to halt hydroelectric development on the New River in the Early 1970s.

5. *The New Resource Economics: The Revelance of Its Core Concepts*
Fundamental to the New Resource Economics critique of contemporary U.S. water policy is a set of assumptions derived from utilitarian social thought. These notions are currently expressed as basic principles of public choice micro- economic theory. They include: (1) reducing collective decisions to individual choice; (2) a utilitarian concept of rationality involving the ranking of value preferences and consistency of choices to maximize values; (3) exchange agreements among individuals (contracts and markets) to adjust individual interests and equitably and efficiently satisfy social welfare requirements; and (4) a highly limited role for government regulation of market processes, functionally restricted to enforcing the legitimacy of contracts legally made through officially sanctioned procedures. These precepts are interactive and mutually reinforcing. We intend to examine each of these precepts in turn, paying particular attention to their limitations as applied to the reform of contemporary water institutions (from: Mumme and Ingram, 1984:6).

REFERENCES

Allison, Graham (1971) *Essence of Decision: Explaining the Cuban Missile Crisis*, Boston: Little Brown and Co., Inc.

Anderson, Terry L. (1983) *Water Crisis: Endign the Policy Drought*, Baltimore: Johns Hopkins University Press.

Ausness, Richard (1983) "Water Rights Legislation in the East: A Program for Reform," *William and Mary Law Review*, 24:546–590.

Congressional Quarterly, Inc. (1981) *Environment and Health*, Washington, D.C.: Congressional Quarterly, Inc.

Ciriacy-Wantrup, S.V. (1975) " 'Common Property' as a Concept in Natural Resource Policy" *Natural Resources Journal*, 15:713–27.

Cox, William E. (1982) "Water Law Primer," *Proceedings*, American Society of Civil Engineers, Vol. 108. New York: ASCE.

Cox, William E. and Shabman, Leonard A. (1985) "A Proposal for Improved Management of Interjurisdiction Water Transfer: *Special Report No. 19*. Blacksburg, Virginia: Virginia Water Resources Research Center.

Gaventa, John (1980) *Power and the Powerlessness: Quiescence and Rebellion in an Appalachian Valley*. Urbana, IL: University of Illinois Press.

Gordon, H. Scott (1954) "Economic Theory of a Common Property Resource: The Fisheries," in *Journal of Political Economy*, 62:124–142.

Griffin, Ronald C. (1984) "Institutionalized Economic Efficiency in Water Allocation." Paper presented at the 20th Annual Meeting of the American Water Resources Association Conference, Washington, D.C., August.

Hardin, Garret (1968) "The Tragedy of the Commons," *Science* 162, 3059 (December 13): 1243–1248.

Howells, David H. and Grigg, Neil S. (1978) *Legal and Administrative Aspects of Water Allocation and Management in North Carolina*, Report No. 133, Raleigh, N.C.: Water Resources Institute of the University of North Carolina.

Hunt, Robert C. and Hunt, Eva (1976) "Canal Irrigation and Local Social Organization," *Current Anthropology*, 17, 3:394–397.

Ingram, Helen M., Laney, Nancy K. and McCain, John R. (1980) *A Policy Approach to Political Representation: Lessons from the Four Corner States*, Baltimore: Johns Hopkins University Press.

Maas, Arthur and Andersen, Raymond (1978) . . . *and the Desert Shall Rejoice: Conflict, Growth and Justice in Arid Environments*, Cambridge, Mass: MIT Press.

Mumme, Stephen P. and Ingram, Helen M. (1984) "Empowerment and the Papago Tribe: Water Politics in Southern Arizona." Paper presented at the Annual Meeting of the American Political Science Association, Washington, D.C., September.

Mumme, Stephen P. and Ingram, Helen M. (1985) "A Comparative Analysis of Three Southwestern Indian Communitites' Participation in Water Resources Decision-Making." Paper presented at the Annual Meeting of the American Political Science Association, New Orleans, LA, September.

Pierce, John C. and Doerksen, Harvey R. (1976) *Water Politics and Public Involvement*, Ann Arbor, MI: Ann Arbor Science Publishers, Inc.

81

Pierce, John C. and Lovrich, Nicholas P. (1980) "Belief Systems Concerning the Environment: The General Public, Attentive Public and State Legislation," *Political Behavior*, 2, 3.

Schoenbaum, Thomas J. (1979) *The New River Controversy* Winston-Salem, N.C.: John F. Blair, Publishers.

Soden, Dennis L. (1985a) "Small-Hydro Development and Public Decision-making" in *Waterpower/'85*. New York, American Society of Civil Engineers.

Soden, Dennis L. (1985b) "Assessing Public Opinion in Subnational Environmental Politics: The Low-Head Hydroelectric Controversy in the Pacific Northwest." Paper presented at the Annual Meeting of the Western Political Science Association, Las Vegas, NV, March.

Soden, Dennis L. (1986) "Public and Collective Goods: A Primer." Mimeo.

Soden, Dennis L. and Wilson, Zaphon R. (1986) "Public Choice in Land and Water Use and Development in Appalachia: A Summary of Research Findings." Paper presented at the 1986 Citadel Symposium on Southern Politics, Charleston, S.C., March.

Trelease, Frank (1954) "Coordination of Riparian and Appropriative Rights to the Use of Water," *Texas Law Review*, 24:24–25.

Trelease, Frank J. (1979) *Cases and Materials on Water Law*. St. Paul, Minn.: West Publishing Co.

U.S. News and World Report (1977) "Is the U.S. Running Out Of Water?," *U.S. News and World Report*, July 18:33.

Walker, William R. and Bridgeman, Phyllis (1985) "Anatomy of a Water Problem: Virginia Beach's Experience." *Special Report No. 18*, Blacksburg, VA:

OLD FURNITURE-NEW ROOMS: THE POETICS OF SPACE IN APPALACHIAN LIT-
ERATURE
    Convenor: Parks Lanier, Radford University
Panelists: Bill Best, Berea College
           Grace Edwards, Radford University
           Nancy Joyner, Western Carolina University
           Parks Lanier, Radford University
           Keith O'dell, Radford Univeristy
           Charlotte Ross, East Tennessee State University
           Melinda Wagner, Radford University

Divine Right And The Red Tent

by
Parks Lanier

Introduction

In a session called "Old Furniture—New Rooms: The Poetics of Space in Appalachian Literature," Bill Best, Grace Edwards, Nancy Joyner, Parks Lanier, Keith O'dell, Charlotte Ross, and Melinda Wagner discussed the significance of land, houses, even particular rooms, in fiction by modern and contemporary Appalachian writers "in search of a usuable past." Typical of the discussion is the essay presented here on Gurney Norman's novel *Divine Right's Trip* (1971), a story which tells how a child of counter-culture comes home to embrace more traditional values in his own unique way. In the new rooms of his heart and mind, Divine Right finds a place for the old furniture—an entire way of life— left him by his Uncle Emmet. How this experience becomes possible is the subject of the study which follows.

In 1966 Edward T. Hall published *The Hidden Dimension*, a book concerned with proxemics, "a term [he] used for the interrelated observations and theories of man's use of space as a specialized elaboration of culture"(1). This important work on how people react and relate to their environment was reviewed in *The Last Whole Earth Catalog* in which Gurney Norman's novel *Divine Right's Trip* first appeared, a novel in which proxemic figures as an important cultural indicator. The *Catalog* review begins with a quotation from Buckminister Fuller, who said, "Don't try to reform man, reform the environment" (182). By the end of Norman's novel, Divine Right is dedicated to environmental reform as president of Magic Rabbit Incorporated, "a scheme to reclaim the soil of the homeplace that had been killed by the strip mining on the slopes above the farm" (Norman 421). He will use rabbit manure and redworms for "soil redemption. Salvation! Healing by miracles, signs and wonders" (Norman 431). Divine Right's birth as a reformer, reclaimer of the environment, comes in a red tent through an encounter with cross-cultural proxemics.

"The Red Tent" is the eighth section of the first part of *Divine Right's Trip*. D.R. and Estelle have just gotten their trip eastward under-way. When they stopped at Eagle Rock State Park,

> The campground was incredibly crowded, but at last [Es-telle] found an empty space...a narrow slot between a GMC pickup...and a green Porsche parked in front of a red pup tent. (Norman 19)

The pickup with the impressive camper on it belongs to William F. Dix-on, a.k.a. The Lone Outdoorsman. The more modest red tent nearby be-longs to two European women, one of whom comes to borrow sugar from Estelle:

> D.R. asked the woman where she got her red tent.
> "You like it?"
> "I've never seen a tent like that before."
> "Would you like to see inside? It is very lovely."
> (Norman 27)

Divine Right accepts and goes inside.

According to what Edward T. Hall has to say about how protective Europeans, especially Germans, are about their private space (135), it seems remarkable that the women would welcome Divine Right into their tent. But camping out has a way of eliminating such barriers; per-haps that explains their hospitable nature. Divine Right's curiosity is also a flattering compliment to two such adventurous and independent wom-en so far from home.

The interior of the red tent is impressive:

> D.R.'s first hit was off the the fantastic quality of the light inside. It was mid-morning by now. The sun was above the tree-line, shining directly into all the little clearings on the western side of the campground. It filled the red tent with the most completely restful light he'd ever seen before. A whole tension that had screwed his face all morning went away as his eyes gulped the quiet rose of the tent's interior. (Norman 27)

In their study *Body, Memory and Architecture*, Bloomer and Moore observe, "The face is truly a facade which acts as an important sign and message system for the body. Facial expressions and activities are metaphors of experiences that can be, or have been, consummated by the body" (43). D.R.'s relaxed face indicates that the red tent has had an immediate salutary effect on his whole body, even though he is in rather cramped quarters:

> It wasn't large at all. There was only one place a person
> oculd half stand up, and two sleeping bags side by side
> would cover most of the floor. Yet somehow it struck D.R.
> as the most spacious, elegant room he'd ever been in. (Norman 27)

On this phenomenon of actual space and perceived space, Bloomer and Moore quote from Geoffrey Scott's *Architecture of Humanism* (1914) concerning the "mechanical, visual, and bodily measures" of a structure:

> In any building three things may be distinguished: the big-
> ness which it actually has [mechanical measurement], the
> bigness which it appears to have [visual measurement], and
> the feeling of bigness which it gives [bodily measure-
> ment]... it is the feeling of bigness which alone has aesthet-
> ic value. (28)

It is precisely this "feeling of bigness" which Divine Right experiences. From outside, the red tent looks small, dwarfed by The Lone Outdoorsman's gigantic GMC camper. From inside, it has a psychic spaciousness which mirrors D.R.'s own expanding consciousness.

D.R. next turns his attention to the tent's interior details:

> It was immaculate. In the corners of the tent near the en-
> trance were two rolled sleeping bags. On top of each bag
> were small blue and white flight bags, both neatly zippered,
> the carrying straps arranged just so. Except for a strip of
> grass down the middle, the ground was covered by two
> straw mats. On each mat was a rubber air mattress, deflated
> and folded into a perfect square and stashed in the far cor-
> ner of the tent. In the middle of the far end stood a short,
> three-legged table with a candle on it, and a single wild-
> flower of some kind, in a glass of water. (Norman 27)

Here in elegant simplicity are displayed the "microcosms of earth, air, fire, and water which renew our recollections of a world inhabited over time, of primal beginnings not yet altogether forgotten" (Bloomer & Moore, 51).

Divine Right responds powerfully to the poetics of the space around him:

> D.R. was amazed. He hadn't smoked any dope in over twelve hours now, and yet he felt completely stoned on the perfect arrangement of the small red world around him... he stretched himself out on one of the mats and stared up at the slanting red roof above him. (Norman 27)

D.R. lies down in order to daydream. "If I were asked to name the chief benefit of the house," says French phenomenologist Gaston Bachelard, "I should say: It allows D.R. to dream in peace, which means that he comes most vitally awake to its potentialities.

Divine Right's experience is not unlike the epiphany of Diogenes Teufelsdrckh in Thomas Carlyle's *Sartor Resartus: The Everlasting Yea*. Diogenes, whose name "born of God" is akin to "Divine Right," awakens from the Center of Indifference to "a new Heaven and a new Earth":

> Beautiful it was to sit there, as in my skyey Tent, musing and meditating; on the high table-land, in front of the Mountains; over me, as roof, the azure Dome, and around me, for fawll, four azure-flowing curtains,—namely, of the Four azure winds, on whose bottom-fringes also I have seen gilding. (Carlyle 129)

For Diogenes, the universe is one great "skyey Tent." D.R. had seen his "spirit-name form" in the clouds above the meadow where he was lying in the grass looking up and breathing deeply in awe of how really simple everything is when you come right down to it" (Norman 11). Now, in the red tent, he rediscovers not only "how really simple everything is," but how everything is "connected." Thomas Carlyle's Diogenes speaks of "organic filaments," exclaiming, "Wondrous truly are the bonds that unite us one and all. . . . I say, there is not a red Indian, hunting by Lake Winnipic, can quarrel with his squaw, but the world must smart for it. . . . It is a mathematical fact that the casting of this pebble from my hand alters the centre of gravity of the Universe" (Carlyle 139). In the red tent, Divine Right the balance freak contemplates such "filaments," intersections to which the whole universe vibrates:

> A tent, he thought. A room of space... marked off and set aside by these walls of red canvas that weren't here yesterday probably and probably won't be here tomorrow, but

86

they are here today and I am here too inside the particular space they enclose. This space has always been here. But it has not always been a room, at least not *this* room, becaus it has never been enclosed by this particular tent before. The space is here. The time is now. And they are intesecting in a way that no other tent has ever caused before. (Norman 29)

In imaginative reverie, Divine Right lies there in the red tent as at the center of a cosmic mandala connected to all things, and connected to himself as the space he occupies connects with the time which is "now."

Into the pool of his imagining Divine Right tosses another pebble:

This very space where I am lying has been tented over before, closed up in other canvas rooms. And so the question seems to be: would another tent around this same space recreate this room, or does this room disappear forever once this red tent has been removed and taken somewhere else? (Norman 29)

Had Gaston Bachelard, in his chapter on shells in *The Poetics of Space*, pursued his musing on the hermit crab "that goes to live in abonadoned shells" (126), he might have answered Divine Right's question. The red tent is not like the nests, drawers, chests, or wardrobes which fascinate Bachelard. It is more like a shell, which may be a moveable house, or a house into which one moves like the hermit crab. But the tent has other attributes, quite unlike the shell:

And what about when this tent is pitched in another place? If you pitch it in the Blue Ridge Mountains, take it down and put it up in the Rockies, has the *same room* been in both places? Or is it another brand new room every time you pitch the tent again? (Norman 29)

With such ephemeral houses Bachelard has nothing to do, nor does Edward Hall concern himself with the proxemics of tents as cultural phenomenon. Bloomer and Moore comment only in passing on the tent's association with "the power of nomadic conquerors" (83). Gurney Norman, however, readily perceives the proxemic values of the red tent, and their cross-cultural significance.

It is important, first of all, that the red tent belongs to Europeans, not Americans. Edward Hall notes that "according to European standards, Americans use space in a wasteful way" (132). In the red tent, however, there is no space wasted. Each occupant has her own space, carefully delineated by the strip of grass between the straw mats. The amenities of life are shared on the little table in the middle. For all its nomadic associations, the tent is civilized by the little flower in a glass of water.

Edward Hall says that Americans in Europe are likely to be uncomfortable with unfamiliar proxemic patterns. The effect of this different pattern on Divine Right, however, is electrifying. In the section following, called "A Place for Everything and Everything in its Place," D.R. is discovered madly cleaning up his space, his "tent," the VW microbus, Urge, who is himself European. Urge had been made in Germany and bought in Germany by an American serviceman. Now fellow Europeans and their immaculately organized red tent are responsible for the first good cleaning Urge has had in ages. In the midst of his work, D.R. exclaims to Estelle,

> This is here and we are now and the intersection of time and space is just special as hell, and I'm going to find out some things we need to know. I believe there's going to be better relations between east and west. (Norman 31)

If Diogenes is right about organic filaments binding the whole world together, then Divine Right's getting "ten cardboard boxes of identical size and [labeling] them with what they're supposed to hold" (Norman 31) will have profound repercussions for world order. As Estelle pitches in to help with the cleaning, D.R. stops her. "Don't throw that glass away," he says. "Here. I'll wash it out after while, I want to put a wildflower in it" (Norman 31). In reading this, one cannot help but think of that famous newsphoto of peace demonstrators putting flowers in soldiers' rifles. Filled with optimism, D.R. says, "I think love and gentleness and neighborliness and human harmony are going to prevail. I think the stars are moving into very particular cosmic arrangements. And we've all got to do our parts. I believe it all depends on everybody doing his part" (Norman 31). What is this but an echo of Carlyle's Diogenes who cried, "Up! up! Whatsoever thy hand findeth to do, do it with thy whole might" (Carlyle 134) and who looked into his own heart for the Promised Land and declared "Americca is here or nowhere" (Carlyle 133).

The experience of the red tent stays with Divine Right all the way to Kentucky where he buries his Uncle Emmet and inherits the rabbit farm. Because the farm hous is threatened by overburden from the stripmine, "a wall of dried mud and shale and blasted rock high as the roof in some places" (Norman 421) which inches forward inexorable as a glacier, D.R. abandons it for the barn, where he plans to "remodel two of the stalls into a weather-tight room, and live in it that winter. . . . If Estelle would come, they would convert the whole end of the barn into a house, and live there together by the rabbits and the worms near the garden" (Norman 425).

The novel ends with Divine Right planning his barn-house, his rabbit farm with thousands and thousands of hutches, and his land reclamation project with rabbit manure. It will come to pass if Estelle comes back to him, and she does. They are married. Perhaps they will live in the barn, or in the VW microbus. Gaston Bachelard says, "Maybe it is a good thing for us to keep a few dreams of a house that we shall live in later, always later, so much later, in fact, that we shall not have time to achieve it. ... It is better to live in a state of impermanence than in one of finality" (61). Swami High-Time from Santa Cruz who officiates at the wedding, refers to his Book of Tao, would have no trouble understanding the French phenomenologist's love of houses still unbuilt. For it all, there is the red tent to thank.

WORKS CITED

Bachelard, Gaston. *The Poetics of Space*. Trans. Maria Jolas. Boston: Beacon Press, 1969.

Bloomer, Kent C. and Charles W. Moore. *Body, Memory, and Architecture*. New Haven: Yale UP, 1977.

Carlyle, Thomas. *Sartor Resartus*. In English Prose of the Victorian Era. Ed. C.F. Harrold and W.D. Templeman. New York: Oxford UP, 1938.

Hall, Edward T. *The Hidden Dimension*. Garden City, N.Y.: Anchor Doubleday, 1969.

Heidegger, Martin. *Being and Time*. Trans. John Macquarrie and Edward Robinson. New York: Harper and Row, 1962.

Merleau-Ponty, M. *Phenomenology of Perception*. Trans. Colin Smith. New York: Routledge and Kegan, 1962.

Norman, Gurney. *Divine Right's Trip*. In *The Last Whole Earth Catalog*. Menlo Park, California: Portola Institute, 1971.

Fiddling in the Poconos: Survival or Revival?[1] [2]

by
John McLaughlin

Scots-Irish settlement of the Appalachian Chain was not confined to its Southern links, but extended from Maryland through Pennsylvania to New York, and from Massachusetts up through Maine. This being the case, one might expect that the distinctive cultural heritage of the Scots-Irish might not be confined to the Southern Mountains, but might also be found in the Northern Appalachians.

But Jan Brunvald's standard introduction to folklore, [The Study of] *American Folklore* (Norton, 1968) identifies seven clear and distinct folklore areas of the United States, among which is Southern Appalachia, with an East-West axis dividing the North across New England (p. 23), and this neatly-drawn map has been picked up by researchers in other fields; for example, Getis, Getis and Fellman's *Human Geography: Culture and Environment* cites "folk cultural maps" from the early works of Glassie, Lomac and Garney (pp. 182–85) which purport to break off the "Southern Backwoods" or "Appalachian Song Family" at the Maryland-Pennsylvania border, with a consequent disjunct Northern and Southern folk heritage.

However, when one finds himself collecting fiddle tunes like "Arkansas Traveler" and "Black Mountain Rag," "Mississippi Waltz" and "Turkey in the Straw" from elderly square dance fiddlers in Northeastern Pennsylvania, he must at least begin to suspect that these early folk cultural maps are in need of some redrawing, along a North-South rather than an East-West axis, perhaps. Maybe there is more to Pennsylvania than the notorious Dutchies, after all.[3]

We begin, then, with the question of whether or not the Scots-Irish fiddle traditions fo the Pocono Mountains of Northeast Pennsylvania—attested to by 93-year-old Papa Jake Miller and 77-year-old Julian Teeple (Interviews, 2/22/86)—has in fact survived two World Wars, the coming of the interstate roads and satellite TV. Or has it merely been given some kind of artificial respiration by outsiders fascinated by the quaint backwoodsmen (analogous to what Burt Feintuch found in Northumbrian small-pipes revivals—AFS paper, Oct. 1985), or by nostalgia buffs seeking to save the children from rock-and-roll (Dick Blaustein, discussion of Missouri Old-Time Fiddlers Associations, AFS paper, Oct. 1985).

If the latter, have some of the well-meaning efforts to restore the fiddler to a place of honor led to unforeseen, even ironic displacements in social function for the fiddling itself, as contests have replaced square-dances as performance venues? When "hot" fiddling wins the prizes, what happens to the fiddler who has spent his performing life providing back-up to a caller? (Interview with Ray Cortwright, 70 year old fiddler for Doc Runsey's Mountain Dewers, with his distaste for "that bluegrass stuff—they play too darn fast!" - 2/20/86).

In fact, Ray Cortwright has never won a fiddle contest in the last twenty years—they go back no further than that in this area of Pennsylvania—and he knows no other old-time square dance fiddler who has won such a contest. I asked him if it were possible that some fiddlers might become discouraged and hang up the fiddle after enough times of that happening, and he answered, "Oh yeah—if I hadn't had the band to play in, I might have done the same thing myself! I mean, I know I'm an alright fiddler—no star or anything like that, y'know—but I know I can fiddle, and I've been playing nigh on forty years like that. So it's not that I can't play. But the judges, y'know, they're influenced by the crowds, the applause, so they don't pay attention to whether the tune's played in the right time or nothing like that. But there's fellas I know who have just give it all up in disgust—'Hell, I guess I ain't no good after all, bud!' " (Interview, 2/20/86).

Asked what the judges should be looking for, Ray answers, "Well, first of all they don't want none of that bluegrass music. I mean, I like it alright myself, like to listen to it and all, but it doesn't—shouldn't—have any place in an old-time fiddle contest. They should be looking for the old tunes, for a start—none of that 'Orange Blossom Special.' They should be looking to make sure they can play a waltz, not just a fast breakdown. And this music is dancing music, like I say—they have got to play it in time, or it's not being done right. At least, as far as I'm concerned." (Interview, 2/2/86).

Papa Jake Miller, who lives in a 12' by 12' foot shack with an outhouse in back, about fifty feet from the edge of a spreading development outside Portland Village, concurs with his younger colleague. "Now, I recall back when there was dancing six nights a week all around here—a body couldn't get to all the dances there was around here! And some of them contests like you have now—some kid who's learnt maybe six tunes in his life gets up there and them judges, some of them don't know their ass from a hole in the ground when it comes to old-time fiddling!" He is quick to assert that he personally has done all right in his day— "But you can see some of these kids got prizes in the contests, and be damned if they could fiddle all night long for a square dance like I done all my young years." (Interview, 2/22/86).

Papa Jake at one time played six nights a week for dancing, 8 pm to 2 am, at the Eagle Valley Corners Inn, near East Stroudsburg, with sets in three different rooms and people waiting to take the dancers places immediately there was a pause between tunes, just him and a caller, all night long, for ten dollars a night, seventeen years in a row, "And I'd get up in the morning and go to work in the quarry as a blacksmith, and all them farmers had to get home and milk their cows." (Interview, 2/22/86). While those glory days may be gone now, he still plays host to young fiddlers who come around to learn tunes and swap stories with him in his shack, which he shares with two lapdogs and his trophies from fiddle contests. On the day of our interview, he had to set straight a visitor who called one of his tunes "The Oil City Quickstep." "Naw it ain't no 'Oil City Quickstep,'" he said. "That there tune was learned by my daddy off this nigger who come up from the South. Didn't have no place to stay, and he was just passing through. So he played us this tune, and my daddy played it after him. And his name was Jimmy the Nigger, so we called that tune its name, and it's Jimmy the Nigger's Tune,' Yes it is. Come from North Carolina, he did. Jimmy the Nigger." (Interview 2/20/86).

The question of origin of repertoire is an interesting if vexed issue, as the preceding anecdote attests. In fact, the tunes played by Papa Jake and Ray Cortwright and Julian Teeple—of whom more later—are standard tunes, to be found in almost any collection of fiddle music, although they may well have been learnt, as Papa Jake's Daddy learnt them, by ear rather than from the printed page, since none of the fiddlers mentioned so far can read a note of music—"Nary a one," says Papa Jake cheerfully.

Julian Teeple, for example, presents an interesting case. A lifelong bachelor, this old man lives alone in a small house a little off a main highway some thirty miles north of Stroudsburg. He has never played for square dancing, although he has fiddled all his life. Too shy to play "out in company," as he puts it, he's a classic example of the "parlor fiddler," who plays for family, friends and fellow-fiddlers, but very rarely in public. "Oh, I might go to the occasional dance, just to hear the fiddler, dont' you know, but then if he wanted to take a break and maybe dance, I'd sit in for a tune or two. But I've never played for a whole dance. It's just not my nature." (Interview, 2/22/86).

However, he has been a keen radio listener all his life—at least, as far back as there was radio—and he was out of these mountains during World War Two, when he was called "Pop" by his outfit, with whom he shared a prisoner-of-war experience he can still remember vividly; along the way, he has befriended a couple of well-intentioned fiddle enthusiasts, who have kept him supplied with records and, now, cassette tapes of fiddle music. As a result, Julian can play you Graham Townsend and Eugene O'Donnell tunes, along with some of the half-remembered English tunes his grandfather brought over from the North of England over a hundred years ago. "Well, you see, whenever I'd get with a fiddler, I'd pick up on his tunes, then the next guy I'd pick up his, and so on and so on. So that means I remember the last ones better than the earlier ones, like you do, so I sometimes can't remember some of the great old tunes. More's the pity." (Interview, 2/22/86).

Among the up-and-coming young fiddlers Julian is in touch with, there is a 29 year old dairy farmer by the name of Steve Jacoby, who is perhaps somewhat more representative—talent aside—of the mainstream fiddling than "Uncle Julian."

Steve is a member of the revivalist organization referred to earlier, the Fred Williams Friends of Old Time Music, which was founded about ten years ago to "preserve and perpetuate" old-time fiddling and Appalachian music. Never mind that the members wear cowboy hats and boots to play, or that the small band within the group—Country Cooking—has a singer whose repertoire is drawn straight from the country-and-western charts. In the words of Andy Cavage, one of the founders, "Fred saw that the old music was dying out—maybe because of rock-and-roll, I don't know—and he determined to keep it alive, to keep it going, and so that's how we got set up in the first place. To have the old music, and to see if maybe we could get the young folks interested in it—something for them to do with their time" (Interview, 1/28/86).

Among the things that they've done with their time is bring Graham Townsend—one of Steve Jacoby's idols—down to the Poconos for concerts at a local high school. I was asked by Steve if I would like to videotape the concert, and, although it was at the time a bit off my taste, I agreed, hoping that serendipity would strike as it so often does when you give it half a chance. The concert was a success, Graham Townsend had no objection to the taping—"for educational purposes"—although he was quick to make it clear to the audience that he had records and cassettes out in the hall to be autographed at intermission, etc. I made the promised copy for the Friends (9/7/85), and thought no more of it until this past April, when I asked if I could travel to a grange social, where the Friends would be playing.

In the middle of the concert, Steve stepped up to the microphone, and announced he was going to do "The Mockingbird." It is the tune, of

93

course, with which Graham Townsend won the World Championships at Sherbourne, in 1962, and with which he had brought his Honesdale audience to their feet the preceding September. With my video camera rolling, Steve then proceeded to produce a near note-perfect copy of Townsend's performance, right down to "patter" and fiddle-taps ("That's a woodpecker!"). As far as I know, Steve Jacoby had never seen Graham Townsend in performance before that September show. On the other hand, he had had the videotape available for study during the following winter months. . . . If I am correct, then, we have a demonstration of how videotaping can enter into the oral processes of tradition, no different in kind than phonograph records or audio-cassettes, but with the added dimension of the visual image for the apprentice fiddler to learn the master's bowing and fingering—and tapping.

In this case, then, it could be argued that I am in no different case than the enthusiasts referred to earlier, who had loaned Julian Teeple cassettes of Irish music and thereby interfered with his memory of English tunes. I stand guilty as charged, I supposed; both cases, in fact, might stand a bit closer scrutiny, since it seems to me that they are perfectly natural processes, no more to be rolled back than the waves for Canute. Indeed, the only caution I would make in situations like this is for the collector to be aware of these and other "interferences" from "outside the tradition." Otherwise, he might collect an item from a fiddler and misidentify its sources, through ignorance of these intervening possibilities.

A case in point might be a tune with a French-Canadian-sounding name, "The Joys of Quebec," which I collected in a session of the Fred Williams Friends of Old Time Music, in their weekly practices. Especially since Andy Cavage had cited French-Canadian as one of the three major ethnic influences in Pocono Mountain fiddling (the others being Scots-Irish and German), I might have been tempted to look further North—let us say to Graham Townsend?—for the source for this tune. But it so happens that it has also been recorded on the June Appal label (out of Kentucky) by the Dutch Cove String Band, among others; could it not also belong among the tunes passed along to Papa Jake by Jimmy the Nigger . . . ?

The point is, of course, that both are clear "possibilities," neither is the exclusive "correct answer," and the collector who insists upon tracking down the sources will have a long and dusty road to travel to get there.

Another caution might also be in order, for the unwary collector in Pennsylvania. There are a number of fiddle contests in this area each year, run as part of local fairs and, more recently, by resort hotels as part of their tourist attractions. At one such—this one run as part of the Greene-Dreher-Sterling fair in Newfoundland last August—I videotaped a dazzling, intricate display of Irish fiddling, by a young man with forearms like hams and thick, short fingers, a swarthy chap wearing a cowboy shirt and the inevitable boots. In fact, he won the contest, with a combination of "Tennessee Waltz," "The Irish Washerwoman," and "Katy Hill." To the neophyte collector—and we have been forewarned that the Governor's Heritage Commission is soon going to be hiring a fresh young Ph.D. to come up into the Northeast and begin fieldworking his way around the mountains—this might have been caputred as a prime example of the revival of fiddling in the Poconos and all that. As it happens, I know this chap from elsewhere. He is Tony De Marco, who was once the fiddler in "Flying Cloud," the house band at the Eagle Tavern in New York City, and a veteran fiddler with two albums of fiddle music—one a twin-fiddling album with Brian Milner—on the market. Tony owns a house in the vicinity, and is a friend of Steve Jacoby, through whom he heard about this new contest, with its prize money waiting for the best in show—which he clearly deserved (Contest videotaped, 8/28/85).

Now, this is not to say that Tony or anyone else should have been "flagged off the track"—although I did hear some mumbling from other young fiddlers about "damned ringers"—it is just to caution the unwary to watch where they are putting their feet before they make too-quick pronouncements concerning the state of the art in fiddling among the Pocono Mountains.

It is with these contests that I would like to close this quick survey of what I have found to be the case so far in my research. Their motives are obviously mixed—to preserve the old-time fiddling, to entertain the tourists until casino gambling is legalized, to enrich the local fair programs —but it is clear that they have taken over from the square dances as public venues for fiddle music in this area. Doc Rumsey's Mountain Dewers may play the local YMCA, and Fred Williams Friends of Old Time Music may play the grange or the local high school; but the prize money, the crowds, in short, "the action," is at the fiddle contests. In theory they are judged by old-timers who know the music; but in fact, as Ray Cortwright somewhat bitterly attests, they are also crowd-pleasers, and the young fiddler who steps right up to the mike and fires off some trick-and-fancy fiddling stands to gain not only an ovation but also the prize money. As noted earlier, this may be having the ironic and unintended effect of disccuraging the very fiddlers whom they were set up to honor and preserve in the first place; for the ego-strokes that we all need, performers especially perhaps, the old-timers have to turn to young enthusiasts, not necessarily well-informed about their music, unless they are fortunate enough to have a Steve Jacoby, who respects their music and will sit in with them at home and play the old tunes with them (Unfortunately bad videotape, with less than minimal lighting, at Julian Teeple's cabin, 11/26/85).

Ignorant crowds are no way to treat old-time square dance music; but if we are not to retreat into the dusty museums, we have to recognize that it is among those ignorant, beer-swilling crowds that we will find our young fiddlers these days. Some, like the aptly-named Johnny Ace, can win in the more traditional settings such as the old-established West End Fair contest (now in its 15th year), with such tunes as "Old Joe Clark" or "Mississippi Waltz," then turn around and walk away with prizes by playing Bill Monroe's "Jerusalem Ridge," at a newer contest the following night (Videotapes, West End Fair, 8/28/85, and Greene-Dreher-Sterling Fair, 8/28/85); Johnny also plays in a hot country band, "Penn Station," which plays at the local resort hotels.

Some, like Steve Jacoby, a member of 4-H and devoted to the farm he lives on, are as at home playing for the grange halls (4/22/86 videotape) as they are running off with the Trick-and-Fancy Division at the West End (8/27/85) or sitting in with their friends in a farmhouse basement for a weekly practice session, where the tunes go around the room and nobody insists on being the star (Videotape at John Wargo's house, Honesdale, PA, 1/28/86).

But that Pocono Mountain fiddling is alive and well is beyond question. That it shares repertoire as well as heritage with the fiddle music of the Southern Appalachians also seems beyond question, although of course the effect of syndicated programs such as "Hee Haw" (referred to admiringly by a number of these fiddlers in passing) cannot be ruled out here, either.3 That it will continue to evolve, under pressures to please the crowds and to satifsy the fiddlers' own love of novelty and variety, there can be little doubt, either. The field has not yet been studied in anything approaching the depth with which, for example, the Southern Appalachians, or even the Central and Southern Pennsylvania traditions have been studied (See the work of Matthew Guntharp and Bob Doyle, *Learning the Fiddler's Ways*, and Samuel P. Bayard's *Hill Country Tunes*). The enticing title of George Korson's early collection of coal-miners' songs, Coal Dust on the Fiddle, threatens to distract us westward to the Scranton coal region before we have fairly begun to evaluate our findings here!

That there is more work ahead, then, goes without saying. That there is room for more workers should be equally obvious (side-comments about newly-hatched Ph.D.s to the side). That the chosen recording medium, 1/2 inch VHS, would eventually lend itself to further circulation, possibly through historical societies' interests in preserving the record of the old-timers, is a suggestion which the current author intends to explore in the near future. Let me say only in closing that I am now in process of exploring the possibility of a folklife conference at my home institution next year (tentative title: "Pocono Foxfire: The Folklife of the Northern Appalachians.") You are invited.4

ENDNOTES

1. The videotapes listed in the "Works Cited" were all obtained through the kind permission of the fiddlers and contest organizers involved, specifically for educational purposes, and with my offer of a souvenir copy gladly accepted, for the recipients' own agendas; one told me quite serenely, in front of her husband, that this would be a good way to remember Pa, especially for the grandchildren, "after he's passed on." Steve Jacoby's use of the Graham Townsend tape is described more fully in the text of this paper. I have oral permission to share these tapes with other investigators, if they would be of any educational value. With that restriction, that they not be re-used other than for research and educational purposes, I will be only too happy to send copies of any of the videotapes listed within the text and cited at the end of the paper, to anyone who will send me a blank 1/2 inch T-120 VHS videotape; it may take some weeks to get your copy back, since it must be copied in "real time" on facilities used for other purposes.

2. I am indebted to Bill Lightfoot of Appalachian State University for the predicate of this title, the emblem of the folk music session within which the videotapes underlying this paper were originally presented at the Ninth Annual Appalachian Studies Conference, Boone, NC, March 22, 1986.

3. I am indebted to Dick Blaustein for a number of things, not least a lively discussion of the North-South re-orientation of Appalachian folklore studies which this paper supports.

4. Recognizing that the name "Foxfire" is of good lineage and is probably copyrighted, I have applied to the Foxfire Fund for their permission to incorporate it into the proposed title of this hoped-for conference. A good title is worth a lot.

WORKS CITED

Bayard, Samuel P. *Hill Country Tunes.* AGS Memoirs, 1944.

Blaustein, Richard. "Missouri Old Time Fiddlers' Associations." Paper
presented at American Folklore Society Convention, Cincinatti, Ohio, October
1985.

Brunvald, Jan H. *The Study of American Folklore: An Introduction.* Norton,
1968.

Feintuch, Burt. "Revivals of Northumbrian Small-Pipes." Paper presented at
AFS Convention, Cincinatti, 1985.

Getis, Arthur, Judith Getis and Jerome Fellmann. *Human Geography:
Culture and Environment.* MacMillian, 1985.

Guntharp, Matthew [and Bob Doyle]. *Learning the Fiddler's Ways.*
Pennsylvania State University Press, 1980.

Korson, George. *Coal Dust on the Fiddle.* Folklore Association, 1965.

VIDEOTAPES COLLECTED

Fred Williams Friends of Old Time Music, at Dreher Grange Hall, So. Sterling, PA, 4/22/86.

Fred Williams Friends of Old Time Music, Practice Session at John Wargo's Farmhouse, Honesdale, PA, 1/28/86.

Graham Townsend at Honesdale High School, Honesdale, PA, 9/7/85.

Greene-Dreher-Sterling Fair Fiddle Contest, Newfoundland, PA, 8/28/85.

Julian Temple, Lord's Valley, PA, 2/22/86.

Papa Jake Miller, Portland, PA, 2/22/86.

Ray Cortwright, Marshalls Creek, PA, 2/20/86.

West End Fair Fiddle Contest, Gilbert, PA, 8/27/85.

The Frank Proffitts, Watauga Folk Artists
"Going Across the Moutains, O Fare You Well"

by
Betsy Covington

Some of America's finest traditional mountain music has been performed by the Proffitts, Frank Sr. and Frank Jr., of Watauga County. More than one hundred twenty folk songs were passed down through the oral tradition in their family and shared with the world through their performance.

Frank Proffitt, Sr. was born on June 1, 1913, in Laurel Bloomery, Tennessee. He was the son of Wiley and Rebecca Creed Proffitt, who moved from Wilkes County, North Carolina to the Cracker Neck section of the eastern Tennessee mountains shortly after the Civil War. When Frank was a young boy the family moved back to North Carolina to the Beaver Dam Section of Watauga County, just a few miles below the Tennessee border.

Frank Proffitt grew up with a deep fascination for the songs sung for generations by his family. The first folklorist to visit and publish songs sung by Frank Proffitt was Frank C. Brown in 1937. Although discovered by Frank Brown, it was the sustained interest in the Proffitts by Frank Warner which gave both Frank Proffitt, Sr. and Frank Jr. the opportunity to perform outside their native mountain area.[1]

In the Autumn 1973 Edition of the *Appalachian Journal* Frank

Warner describes his first visit to Beech Mountain, when he went to get a dulcimer from Nathan Hicks:

> It was June 5, 1938, when we first reached the house on Beech Mountain. A crowd of some twenty-five kinfolk and neighbors were waiting for us—with guitars, home-made banjos, dulcimers, fiddles, and French harps. The best singer and guitar player among them turned out to be Nathan's son-in-law, Frank Proffitt, who had walked ten miles across the mountains from his home in Pick Britches Valley to sing with us.[2]
>
> Before long everybody was making music. The sound and the people, that afternoon gave us a feeling we have never lost. It was the beginning of our life-long interest in traditional music and the people who remember it. We had not come with the idea of collecting songs, but Anne couldn't help taking down in shorthand the words of three songs Frank Proffitt sang: "Dan Doo," a version of the Child ballad, "The Wife Wrapt in Wetherskin;" "Moonshine," a story about the effect of homemade liquor; and "Hang Down Your Head, Tom Dooley."...[3]

"Tom Dooley" became part of Frank Warner's repertoire; and when he sang it, he told the story of collecting it from Frank Proffitt. Frank had learned it from his father, who had learned it from his mother, Adeline Perdue, who had been aquainted with Tom Dula when she lived in Wilkes County. In 1868 she had journeyed with her brother to Statesville to see Tom and to go to his hanging. She said she heard him singing the song about himself while sitting in his jail cell. She learned it and sang it throughout her life.[4]

"Tom Dooley"

Hang your head, Tom Dooley. Oh, hang your head and cry.
Killed little Laurie Foster. Poor boy, you're bound to die.
CHORUS: Hang your head, Tom Dooley,
               Hang your head and cry,
               Hang your head, Tom Dooley,
               Poor boy, you're bound to die.

I met her on the mountain, And there I took her life.
I met her on the mountain, And stobbed he with my knife.

CHORUS

Hand me down my banjo, I'll pick it on my knee.
This time tomorrow, It'll be no use to me.

CHORUS

This time tomorrow, Reckon where I'll be.
Down in some lonesome valley, Hanging on a white oak tree.

CHORUS[5]

Frank Warner taught "Tom Dooley" to Alan Lomax, who published it in *Folk Song U.S.A.* in 1947. It was the *Folk Song U.S.A.* copyrighted version which was recorded on Capitol Records by the Kingston Trio in 1958. The song rose to the top of the charts and sold over three million copies.

It was during their beginning popularity that the Proffitts witnessed the Kingston Trio in concert on television. When Frank Proffitt, Sr. heard them singing "Tom Dooley" and saw them swinging their hips and cutting up, he felt sick at heart. Tears came into his eyes, and he went outside to think it over. It just did not seem respectful to the memory of Laurie to sing their story in such a flippant manner.[6]

Believing that they, too, should share in the royalties, Frank Warner, Alan Lomax and Frank Proffitt sued Capitol Records. This was the first case of rights being claimed to a copyrighted folk song, so there was no clear-cut precedent to follow. After many months of negotiating, an out-of-court settlement gave Warner, Lomax and Proffitt the rights to the song from 1962 on.[7]

Speaking of that time in their lives Frank Proffitt, Jr. says, "My father was satisfied for the way the settlement came out. He thought it was selfish to wish for more than he needed to make it. He was a humble man."[8]

Though the royalties did not approach the earnings during the time of its greatest popularity, they made a significant improvement in the lifestyle of the Proffitts. The first check which came was for $700.00, and bought food and new shoes for the family. The most money which came in yearly was four to five thousand dollars, but seldom was it that much.

Along with the money came recognition and interest from the public. Newspapers and magazines came to interview, and others came to visit. Orders for homemade fretless banjos and dulcimers Frank had learned to make from his father increased. He was surprised and pleased that people from all over appreciated the traditional music he knew so intimately.

It was through the friendship of Frank Warner that Frank Proffitt received his first invitation to perform outside the North Carolina moun-

101

tains in 1961. The University of Chicago was holding its first Folk Festival. Frank Proffitt referred to himself as a "shy mountain man;" it took a lot of encouragement and soul-searching for him to be willing to go. He felt he was coming apart at the seams, yet he was proud that others appreciated "the simple things" and respected the mountain culture. He felt he should do anything he could to preserve the music of his people. This was a top priority with him, and it was what enabled him to overcome his timidity.

He journeyed across the mountains to Chicago to the Folk Festival. While waiting to go on stage, he observed the performance of some "blue-grass boys" in cowboy hats and wondered about his plain clothes. He questioned if needed a white sparkling tuxedo or something to "give it an extra lick." He decided what he had to offer was himself and his traditions, so he would go out and do it the old way. Frank sang, and the audience was charmed. They gave him a standing ovation. There was much joking as to whether Frank saw the audience standing, being the spotlights had been turned up and the audience lights lowered to help him overcome his stagefright.[9]

Even when he received great acclaim he did not "let it go to his head." He remained the same "shy mountain man." When he was asked once why he did not change, he replied, "I wouldn't know what to change to."[10] He wanted to be a representative of his kind of people, never to exalt himself.[11]

Sandy Paton was so impressed by the talent and authenticity of Frank Proffitt that he wanted to record him for Folkways Records. He took recording equipment from New England to Watauga County and recorded him at home. The resulting album was *Frank Proffitt Sings Folk Songs* (1962 copyright). Recording Frank at home in 1961 was the inspiration from which came the founding of Folk-Legacy Records. Folk-Legacy's first album was by Frank Proffitt. *Frank Proffitt, Reese, North Carolina* (1962 copyright). It was made from tapes recorded in that winter of 1961. A later *Memorial Album* (1968 copyright) formed a total of three sound recordings of Frank Proffitt.[12]

From 1961 to 1965 was a period of significant activity in Frank Proffitt's musical career. He was invited to a number of colleges, universities, and festivals. Some of the places he performed were the Pinewoods Music Camp, Berea College, the Newport Folk Festival and the 1964 World's Fair. He received the Burl Ives Award in 1963 for his two-finger method of banjo picking.[13]

Frank Proffitt died suddenly in his sleep, November 22, 1965 at age fifty-two. He had been to Charlotte to take his wife, Bessie, for an operation. After he drove back home, he went to bed and did not awaken. He was buried in the Milsap cemetery at Bethel, not far from his home, after the memorial service at Bethel Baptist Church.[14]

To raise money for a tombstone, Frank Warner organized a concert at Hunter College in New York City in 1966. Among those singing were Doc Watson, Jean Ritchie and Pete Seeger. A granite marker was erected in 1967.[15] The family suggested the words of one of Frank's songs to be engraved into the headstone, "Going Across the Mountain, O Fare You Well."

The song "Going Across the Mountain" is a Civil War song which came to Frank Proffitt through his father, Wiley Proffitt. Wiley's father, John Proffitt, had been one of those to go join the Union Army in Tennessee.[16]

"Going Across the Mountain"

Going across the mountain, Oh, fare you well;
Going across the mountain, You can hear my banjo tell.

Got my rations on my back. My powder it is dry;
I'm a-going across the mountain. Chrissy, don't you cry.

Going across the mountain To join the boys in blue;
When this war is over, I'll come back to you.

Going across the mountain, If I have to crawl.
To give old Jeff's men A little taste of my rifle ball.
Way before it's good daylight, If nothing happens to me,
I'll be way down yander In old Tennessee.

I expect you'll miss me when I'm gone, But I'm going through;
When this war is over, I'll come back to you.

Going across the mountain, Oh, fare you well;
Going across the mountain, You can hear my banjo tell.[17]

Frank and Bessie Hicks Proffitt had six children, and one of them, Frank, Jr., is a folk musician in the same tradition of his father. Born Franklin Benjamin Proffitt on September 8, 1946, Frank learned to play when he was ten years old. He worked on it secretly to pass the time, listening to his father's records and imitating him. When his father caught him practicing, he was surprised and pleased that he played so well.[18]

His first trip to play in concert with his father was to Berea College in 1965. Since then, he has performed at the 1969 Newport Folk Festival, the 1982 World's Fair, the summer festivals at the Smithsonian Institute and many other gatherings. He has been making a living with his music since 1978. He became an "artist in the schools" through the North Carolina Arts Council at that time.[19] For this year 1985–86 he is the artist-in-residence at Western Piedmont Community College in Morganton.

Frank Proffitt, Jr. is a delightful storyteller, as well as musician. He says his storytelling comes from the Hicks side of the family. His mother's cousins, Stanley and Rey Hicks, renowned storytellers, told him many tales as he was growing up. These tales about Jack and his adventures are retold humorously and artfully to Frank's audiences.[20]

Considering his talents a gift from God, Frank is appreciative for his heritage. In speaking of his father he says, "I was proud of him and wanted to be a part of it—the magic and wonderment of it all. I still feel that way."[21]

ENDNOTES

1. Personal interview with Frank Proffitt, Jr., 12 April 1983.

2. Anne and Frank Warner. "Frank Noah Proffitt: Good Times and Hard Times on the Beaver Dam Road." *Appalachian Journal.* Autumn 1973, pp. 164–165.

3. *Ibid.*

4. Personal interview with Frank Proffitt, Jr., 24 August 1985.

5. *Ibid.*

6. Frank Proffitt, Jr., "Mountain Music Concert." McAllister School Auditorium, Concord, North Carolina, 14 February 1983.

7. Proffitt, personal interview, 25 August 1985, *Ibid.*

8. *Ibid.*

9. *Ibid.*

10. *Ibid.*

11. Warner, *Ibid.*, p. 175.

12. Sandy Paton, Jacket Notes, *Frank Proffitt Memorial Album*, Folk-Legacy Records, 1968.

13. Personal interview with Frank Proffitt, Jr., 2 May 1983.

14. *Ibid.*

15. Warner, *Ibid.*, p. 191.

16. Proffitt, personal interview, 2 May 1983, *Ibid.*

17. Frank Proffitt, "Going Across the Mountain," *Frank Proffitt*, Folkways Records, 1962.

18. Telephone interview with Frank Proffitt, Jr., 15 February 1986.

19. Proffitt, personal interview 25 August 1985, *Ibid.*

20. Proffitt, personal interview 2 May 1983, *Ibid.*

21. Proffitt, telephone interview, 15 February 1986, *Ibid.*

REFERENCES

Paton, Sandy. Jacket Notes, *Frank Proffitt Memorial Album.* Folk-Legacy Records, 1968.

Proffitt, Frank, Jr. "Mountain Music Concert." McAllister School Auditorium, Concord, North Carolina. 14 February 1983.

Proffitt, Frank, Jr. Personal interview. 12 April 1983.

Proffitt, Frank, Jr. Personal interview. 2 May 1983.

Proffitt, Frank, Jr. Personal interview. 25 August 1985.

Proffitt, Frank, Jr. Telephone interview. 15 February 1986.

Warner, Anne and Frank. "Frank Noah Proffitt: Good Times and Hard Times on the Beaver Dam Road." *Appalachian Journal* (Autumn 1973):162–193.

Somewhere Over Beech Mountain: Contemporary Appalachian Artifacts and The Land Of Oz

by
Charles Alan Watkins

The Land of Oz was a theme park based on the L. Frank Baum Oz characters atop Beech Mountain in Avery County, Western North Carolina. Its birth in 1970 was intertwined with the land rush and concomitant ski boom that occurred in the mountains during the decade of the 1960's, and its demise in 1980 reflected the fallout from financial woes that the ski and second home industries suffered in the early 1970's. In the summer of 1985 and throughout 1986 Appalachian State University's new museum facility, the Appalachian Cultural Center, acquired a large number of significant artifacts from The Land Of Oz to serve as a centerpiece for its planned exhibition on the history of tourism in the mountains. The acquisition and announced plans to exhibit the Oz material has brought into focus a number of questions that museums of Appalachia will increasingly have to deal with, and Oz makes an interesting case study by which to examine these questions.

To understand the Land of Oz, one must first consider its parent company, the Carolina Carribbean Corporation (CCC). The genesis of CCC occurred in 1964 when Grover and Harry Robbins, two Watauga county natives, purchased a large tract of land atop Beech Mountain from Dr. Thomas H. Brigham, a Birmingham, Alabama dentist who had been influential in developing skiing as a sport in Western North Carolina. The Robbins Brothers had gotten their start in the sawmill and lumber business but increasingly their interests turned to tourism and resort development. Their father Grover Robbins, Sr., had owned and operated the original Blowing Rock tourist attraction in Blowing Rock, and Harry Robbins recalled that his first job had been to put Blowing Rock bumper stickers on visitors' cars. In 1956 they began to develop Tweetsie Railroad as a theme park and this was followed in 1964 by construction of Hound Ears, a second home and golf resort between Boone and Linville, North Carolina.

What Grover and Harry Robbins envisioned atop Beech Mountain made their other enterprises pale by comparison, however. In 1964 they formed the Carolina Carribbean Corporation, so named because their North Carolina resort was to be linked with a condominium development, The Reef, in St. Croix, the Virgin Islands. Property owners on Beech would have membership in the Carolina Carribbean Club and would have priveleges at the St. Croix development. An airline was envisioned that would shuttle people back and forth between Beech Mountain and the Carribbean, as well as pick up skiers from various locations in the Southern United States.

At heart, CCC's business on Beech Mountain was to sell resort and second homesites. Grover Robbins had unlimited faith in the area, stating that, "For years to come, the best things will be happening in Western North Carolina's mountains. . . . It is inevitable . . . for this is the best place of all." The Robbins' believed that vacation homes were within the reach of many Americans, and the CCC desigend a model "cottage" that could be built for $13,500-$14,500. Presumably this cottage would appeal to the same sort of people who drove Volkswagens and was therefore, dubbed Volkshause.

All of the amenities at Beech were simply inducements to purchase one of the 4,000 planned homesites, and there were amenities to spare. CCC planned to offer two 18 hole golf courses, one 9 hole course, horsetrails, streams and man made lakes for trout fishing and an area for bird hunting. CCC even hired famed coach Paul Dietzel to develop a family fitness program for Beech residents.

The major attraction, however, was a series of ski slopes at the top of the mountain. As land scales were at the true center of CCC, skiing was at the company's promotional center—it was the flagship activity of the resort and the one that made land purchase attractive. Because skiing was a promotional activity at Beech rather than part of the business, it was never really expected to make a profit and apparently it never did under CCC management.

Nevertheless, the plant investment in skiing was enormous, and the corporation wished to be able to use the chair lift and gondola systems in the summer also. For that reason, CCC planned for a small theme park at the very top, the Pinnacles. To that end, a young Charlotte designer, Jack Pentes was brought to the mountain. Pentes had done other work for the Robbins brothers. In addition to redesigning the Blowing Rock, Pentes' firm had also done much of the design work at Tweetsie and a small history gallery of the Green Park Inn, at that time a Robbins property. Pentes remembers that the idea of recreating Oz came to him as soon as he reached the top of Beech, "Those beautiful trees all seemed to have faces, . . . and their limbs seemed to be reaching out for me. Then I saw a cave and realized it was the Cowardly Lion's cave—just where it should be. It was over the rainbow—part of another world." By February 1967, plans were sufficiently underway for CCC to announce that a tourist attraction called the Land of Oz would be included in the development. Oz opened officially on June 15, 1970 and was fully operational on July 3.

As planned by Pentes, the park was truly a vest-pocket park, comprising only about sixteen acres, of which seven were left undeveloped. Visitors to the park had the option of riding one of the ski lift systems to the top of the mountain where the park was located or riding a specially painted bus to the top. Once there visitors first toured the L. Frank Baum Museum which exhibited a number of costumes, props and articles of furniture from the MGM auction that was held on May 17, 1970 to raise funds to build the MGM Grand Hotel in Las Vegas. From the museum, visitors were taken to the Judy Garland memorial overlook which offered a dramatic view of the Elk Valley far below. Then came Uncle Henry and Auntie Em's farm that included a Gothic style farmhouse, barn and some outbuildings. Crops were actually cultivated at the farm and there was a petting zoo of farm animals, sponsored by Purina, in the barn area. Visitors were then taken in groups for a tour of the farmhouse. While inside, the people were suddenly informed that a cyclone was on the way and that they should all go to the cellar. In the cellar, they were treated to a rear screen projection of a cyclone, actually made of a film of water being stirred in a bucket with superimposed effects, and appropriate sound effects.

When the all-clear was given, the visitors were told that they were being taken back into the house, but instead they were led into a duplicate house built onto the back of the original and one story lower. This house was an exact duplicate of the other one including the furniture, but here things were in disarray—chairs thrown about, tables turned over, pictures askew. To give the effect that the house was no longer on flat land, Pentes designed the floors to be built at a slope, an effect that made visitors stagger drunkedly out the door toward Oz. Outside, the legs of the wicked witch could be seen sticking out from the house where it had

108

supposedly landed on her. Visitors then proceded down the yellow brick road, constructed of specially made bricks with a yellow glaze on the upper surface. They went through Munchkin Land featuring small Munchkin houses and some 500 Mushrooms, all made of sprayed foam. Along the way, the visitors met the other Oz characters—the Scarecrow had his own little house from which he emerged to lip-sync his greeting to the visitors, then do a song and dance routine. Similarly, the tin man performed in front of another house while the visitors watched from an overlook gazebo, and the lion appeared from his den to perform his own special routine. The Wicked Witch was next and her song, also lip-synced, made it clear that she was a harmless bumbler who could not get the recipes right for her magic potions. At the end of the road came Emerald City, consisting of a group of buildings that served as a theater, shop and office area. Here, miniskirted Munchkin girls distributed Greenie Glasses, made of cardboard and colored plastic, to the tourists so that they could view Oz in the proper hue. At set intervals, a stage show, the "Magic Moment," took place. In this, the tour's grand finale, the various Oz characters met the Wizard, actually a rear screen projection of opera star John Richards McCrae, received their hearts' desire and watched Dorothy disappear in one of the balloons that comprised an aerial ride around the park, each balloon suspended from a converted chair lift system. The shops sold items such as Oz Cream, a specially designed ice cream that had green chunks of candy in it.

Pentes was determined that his park would be an original and he refused to copy from the film, "The Wizard of Oz." He brought together a remarkable team that relied heavily on home grown talent. Music for the park was written by Charlotte composer Loonis McGlohon and Alec Wilder whose songs had been recorded by the likes of Frank Sinatra and Tony Bennett. The only song that remained from the film was "Over the Rainbow." One of the vocalists, Lorri Ham, later recorded "I'd Like To Teach The World To Sing." Charlotte sculptor Austin Fox created the costume designs for the Oz characters and the sculpture of Dorothy and Toto that was used in the Judy Garland memorial overlook. Fox had earlier gained success as the sculptor of the Femlin characters for Playboy. Costumes were made by Brooks Van Horne, the New York theatrical costumer. Hollywood choreographer Alice Leggett laMar created special dances for each character and choreographed the "Magic Moment" stage show. Pentes even specially designed the souvenirs that were to be sold in the shops in Emerald City.

The hard work paid off. The Land of Oz won the annual Washington, D.C. Daily New Award for the year's outstanding tourist attraction. According to Myron Glaser, manager of Resort and Travel News for the Scripps-Howard newspaper, the Land of Oz was "the hands down winner." Glaser described the park as "exquisite" and said "We've never seen a more beautiful natural setting nor a finer marriage of a place and an idea. It is truly an adventure, imaginative and unspoiled." The award was decided upon even before the balloon ride was completed—that ride opened on July 3. The park attracted over 400,000 people that first year and it became the state's leading tourist attraction almost overnight.

Just as fast, though, the fortunes of the park began to decline. According to Tom Seig who served as a publicist for Oz,

> "Commercialization by Carolina Caribbean Corp., the original owner, had begun the second year, when people's shoes began to stick on ice-cream wrappers and cotton-candy cones on the Yellow Brick Road. The hawkers had come to Oz, and so had Japan and Taiwan, souvenirs would no longer be tailored to the story and park, and the emerald-studded Oz cream would become plain ice cream. Everything would be cheapened by the price of admission."

At heart, Carolina Carribbean was in trouble. Beginning in 1971, the tightening economy began to work against the Company. Inflation pushed interest rates high and damaged second home sales. The gas crunch of 1974 exacerbated conditions, and heavily crippled tourism. Further, a series of mild winters from 1971 through 1973 severely damaged the ski business. This overall downturn pushed all the Western North Carolina land sale/ski developments to the wall, but CCC was especially vulnerable. Grover Robbins had died in 1970 but the projects he had spun off, including the Dominican Corporation, a resort city on the coast of the Dominican Republic, a camper park enterprise called Land Harbors and Walden, a planned community near Charlotte, were all subject to the same forces affecting CCC, thereby increasing the pressure on the Beech development. Then in September, 1972 machine gun-weilding terrorists killed four people on the Fountain Valley Golf Course in St. Croix. That effectively ended any profitablity that the Reef might have had. the company reported that it lost over $6 million in the first nine months of FY 1973 and $9 million in FY 1974. The company sought cutbacks and by August 1974 was listing the Land of Oz as one property being considered for sale. But it was too late. On November 25, 1974 the U.S. Securities and Exchange Commission ordered trading suspended in CCC stock.

In February 1975 CCC reorganized in an effort to stave off bankruptcy but it closed down operations in September 1975. On October 31, 1975 a judge ordered planned liquidation of the assets of CCC but the Beech Mountain Property Owners Association leased the village and restaurant and the skiing facilities for the winter of 1975–76. The title to The Land Of Oz passed to the mortgage holder, Tri South of Atlanta, Georgia.

110

The trouble for Oz had just begun, however. On December 28, 1975 a fire at Oz destroyed the theatre, along with all the costumes and audio visual material. The museum was vandalized and a number of artifacts including the dress Judy Garland wore during the filming of the Wizard of Oz were stolen. Tri South vowed to reopen Oz and it did so with a number of changes.

These changes, perhaps based upon sound managerial practice, tore at the heart of Jack Pentes' concept. No longer would there be an elaborate stage show with rear screen projection. Now there would be a live Wizard and a puppet show. Replacement costumes were ordered not from Brooks van Horne but from a Charlotte costumer who closely followed the styles of the film. Oz continued operation until 1980 when Jack Pentes was called to assess what it would take to do Oz really well again. Pentes reported that $165,000 would have to be spent immediately and $1,000,00 soon thereafter to update Oz. In Pentes' mind, the alternative to spending the money was to close the park altogether.

Beech Mountain officials chose the latter course and the 1980 season was the last for Oz. Beech Mountain officials found it difficult to stop vandalism of the park that began soon after Oz was shut down. People threw bricks throughthe styrofoam faces on the trees and denuded the witch's castle of it crennelation. Antiques from Dorothy's house disappeared along with most of the 500 mushrooms. By 1985 the park was in ruin.

Yet amid that ruin had been a dream. "It was supposed to be magic," said Jack Pentes, "and it was magic, I think, the first year." But it was a magic that could have happened in the mountains, and in virtually every respect, Oz was a mountain project—built by mountain people for owners who were themselves mountain people. The park's design was in part dictated by the availability of local skills such as stonemasonry, and eve the Birdhouse Tree was constructed by the famed blacksmith, Daniel Boone V. The employees were kids from the surrounding area, and the existence of the park itself symbolized the change in the regional economy from farming to tourism. Nothing could better illustrate this change than a comparison between the CCC side of the mountain and Beech Mountain's other side, the eastern slope in Watauga County, which had been virtually inaccessible until quite recently. Folk scholars and musicologists had long recognized this area as one in which certain family such as the Hicks' and the Presnell's, had held onto older traditions. It was, therefore, highly symbolic of modern Appalachian change that both Munchkins and pre-industrial mountaineers simultaneously inhabited the same mountain.

Yet when the Appalachian Cultural Center began to acquire objects from the park, a number of people reacted unfavorably to Oz, questioning what relevance a theme park had to Appalachia. This should not have been surprising since even our national museum is occasionally faced with similar criticism. When for example, the Smithsonian's National Museum of American History received the Archie Bunker chair and the Fonz's leather jacket, the museum became involved in a "storm of controversy" because "virtually no one outside the collecting division [of the Museum] perceived any cultural relevance whatsoever in preserving these items." It was clear that the Appalachian Cultural Center was in somewhat a similar bind. In rethinking the appropriateness of acquiring Oz, the Center developed some cautionary guidelines that served, not only to place Oz into perspective, but also a good deal of contemporary Appalachian material culture as well. These include:

1. Don't let the collection run the museum.

Museum collections are obviously based on objects that have survived to the present day and yet within that pool of surviving artifacts some are considered better than others. As one museum authority notes, certain objects tend to be " 'preselected' by time and consensus." In the instance of Appalachian artifacts, time has been a significant factor since the hardiest objects—those made of metal, for example—tend to last, while paper items usually disappear quickly. This means that what survives from a culture may not be the most representative or descriptive of objects, such as early kitchen implements and farm tools, were ubiquitous in rural America and are not specifically Appalachian at all. When such artifacts are exhibited in a context that refers to them as uniquely Appalachian—either overtly or implied—the our understanding of the nature of the region is severely skewed.

Magnifying this problem is the inability of the region's museums to move beyond the paradigm of Appalachia that was establhlished by cultural entrepreneurs of all sorts over the past century. The tenents of this belief system are well-known and include such concepts as "pioneers in an industrial age," "the romance of log cabin living," "craft work for spiritual uplift," "carefree muscians," and "the land that time forgot." this is a paradigm that is repellent but attractive too because the ojects that fit the scheme—dulcimers, period log cabin interiors, crafts of all sorts—are themselves compelling and lend themselves to the story so well. But now it is time that the region's museums either use the old objects to tell a new story or find altogether a new set of objects. Mountain culture is simply too rich and varied to allow material survivals or the canonization of certain objects to dictate how the story of the region will be told.

2. Many objects have multiple meanings.

A single object can be significant in a variety of contexts, each one emphasizing a different aspect of the object's meaning. Increasingly, museums in Appalachia must reach beyond the standard interpretation of their collections if they are to make a contribution to the understanding of their region. For example, the hand tool in a museum's collection may have been purchased from a general store, an idea that brings into focus many questions about the meaning of the store itself and the concept of puchasing in the mountains. How did the original owner acquire the object—with money or by barter? Who owned the store and what was its influence on the community. Do records from the store make a comment on the idea of isolation in the region? When thoughts such as these are considered, perhaps where the tool came from is more important than the tool itself.

In the case of Oz, the Center acquired Uncle Henry's large farm tools—the hay rake and seeder that stood in front of the barn. On one level these were used as props for an amusement park but they were also purchased by the park's designer from farmers sho had used them on Beech Mountain. Again, these objects have meanings within meanings.

In this vein it is useful to remember the baseball player Ritchie Ashburn who was once in a hitting slump and decided that, metaphysically, something was wrong. Ashburn began to take his bat to bed with him and when asked why, he replied that he wanted to get to know his bat better. I suggest that, like Ritchie Ashburn, museums need to get to know their objects better.

3. Don't get hung up on the past when interpreting the past.

In the search for the old and the rare objects of a perceived Appalachian heritage, museums stand in danger of losing the objects of today which may even be more useful in broadly interpreting the culture of this region. While we do surveys of log buildings, we pay little attention to the significance of kit rnach houses that everywhere surround us. In the same vein, we celebrate the early craft of heritage of the region but overlook the folk iconography of many roadsigns for Baptist churches, which are frequently in the shape of churches.

Recently the Center acquired a large sign that had been used by a wholesale nursery and greenery dealer. On it was a painting of a primeval mountain forest that is certainly the rival of anything done by artists such as Eliot Dangerfield or William Frerichs in portraying the majestic scenery of the region. It is however only some 20 years old and barely escaped the owner's chainsaw. Dangerfield landscapes are expensive and rare but contemporary depictions of the forest are neither, and museums may find that to get at the past, contemporary objects may serve well.

4. Establish a purchase fund.

Even contemporary objects cost money and museums without funds to acquire objects are at a serious disavdantage if they are seriously attempting to develop a collection designed to tell a specific story or to follow an interpretational concept. As Edith Mayo, Associate curator in the Smithsonian's dividison of Political History puts it,

> "collecting wihtout funding doubles the problems of acquisition. It usually takes great persuasion to convince individuals or groups to part with objects for which they feel personal attachment, or items that embody a commitment central to their lives. It is even more difficult to acquire those objects without offering compensation."

This is not to say that our regional museums will not continue to receive valuable and useful gifts. It must be recognized, though, that rising prices for antiques and collectables put great pressure upon people of middling financial circumstances to sell pieces rather than to give them away. A tax deduction is not much inducement to people who are working to make ends meet.

Thus the museum must compete in the marketplace with dealers and private collectors for the best pieces. The advantage is that as museums redefine what Appalachian artifacts are, they will automatically have first crack at the best examples since it will be the museums themselves that will first call attention to some of these objects as valuable and collectible objects. Many of these objects should and will be contemporary. For example, many of the Oz souvenirs that can still be found in flea markets in the Boone area are expected to rise in value when the Oz exhibition opens.

5. Let us not abdicate our professional responsibilities.

The field of material culture was developed in museums and it is in museums that the field is practiced best. Today, only television rivals the museum as an interpreter of history for the public and museums are doing a far better job of it than the mighty cathode. This means that museums, and especially Appalachian museums, should never act like ships adrift, sailing at the whim of pervailing wind, waiting for published scholarship to point the way. They should be an active force in the reconstruction and the reorganizing of the past.

Most importantly, museums of Appalachia must stop following the paradigm of the region imposed by an outside culture. It is this paradigm that leads museums to laud Doris Ulmann photographs when Appalachia's real story is in the family albums of the people who lived here. It leads to a romantic appreciation of split rail fences while John Ward of Watauga Falls, North Carolina—a man who held international patents for a portable fence he invented—is forgotten. And it leads to a belief that The Land Of Oz, though built and staffed by mountain people and located on one of the highest mountains in Western North Carolina, somehow is not Appalachian. But Oz existed and still does—in a museum and in memory—and as S. Dillon Ripley, former Secretary of the Smithsonian Institution said, "In this brave new world of ours, perhaps only objects which inherently possess truth can teach truth."

ENDNOTES

1. My discussion of Carolina Carribbean Corporatoin is based on material contained in the clipping files of the Appalachian Collection, Appalachian State University. The appropriate files are entitled "Skis and Skiing," "Land of Oz," "Robbins, Harry and Grover," and "Beech Mountain, N.C."

   For two good summary articles about CCC see "Robbins' Brothers Start $8 Million Recreation Project," *Watauga Democrat*, February 2, 1967, "Robbins, Harry and Grover" file and "New Ski Resort Opens This Week," *Winston-Salem Journal*, December 22, 1967, "Skis and Skiing" file.

2. The basis of the material on Jack Pentes comes from a number of interviews with Jack Pentes, Ruth Pentes and Tom Seig. A good overview of Jack Pentes' role can be found in Tom Seig, "Land of Oz Crumbles," *Winston- Salem Journal*, May 19, 1985, pp. C1 and C6.

   Another interesting view of Pentes and The Land Of Oz can be found in Aljean Haremetz, *The Making of the Wizard of Oz*, New York: Limelight Editions, 1984, pp. 297–8.

3. "Follow the Yellow Brick Road," n.p., n.d., "Land of Oz" file, Appalachian Cultural Center, ASU.

4. "Oz Gets National Award," n.p., n.d., Clipping in "Land of Oz" file, Appalachian Cultural Center, ASU.

5. Seig, "Land Of Oz Crumbles."

6. Ibid.

7. Edith P. Mayo, "Contemporary Collecting," *History News*, October 1982, p. 10.

8. Mayo, "Contemporary Collecting," p. 9.

9. Ibid., p. 11.

10. Ibid., p. 9.

CPSIA information can be obtained
at www.ICGtesting.com
Printed in the USA
LVOW05s1802110717
540988LV00021B/337/P

9 781469 636788